"This is a useful and e
in a field often fraught
complements much e
gathers it together to suggest an integrated art therapy practice.

—*Dr. Marian Liebmann, OBE, art therapist,*
*lecturer, workshop leader, and author*

"As a proponent of cultural competence, I applaud Dr. Jackson's paradigm, which shifts the discourse from proficiency to humility. The transformative reflective perspectives and art experientials enhance art therapists' appreciation of the attributes of cultural humility. Required reading for anyone committing to lifelong self-reflection, equitable patient–practitioner interactions, and social action."

—*Cheryl Doby-Copeland, PhD, ATR-BC, LPC, LMFT,*
*HLM, clinical program coordinator, Parent Infant*
*Early Childhood Enhancement Program, adjunct*
*faculty member, GW Art Therapy Program*

"Louvenia Jackson's *Cultural Humility in Art Therapy* proposes cultural humility as a way of being that positions, develops, and integrates art therapy professionals as spiritual, political, and creative beings. At its best this book offers up practical pathways through this complex world of authentic engagement with diverse clients in this age of social justice. Vital for BAME practitioners, useful for all."

—*Jean Campbell, artist educator*

"Cultural competence is conceptualized as a way of doing. Cultural humility is conceptualized as a way of being. This book offers insight into new paradigms in thinking. Acquiring cultural competence and engaging diverse clients with cultural humility ensures that their identities will be respected within the practice of art therapy."

—*Stella A. Stepney, MS, ATR-BC, LCAT,*
*Saint Mary-of-the-Woods College*

*of related interest*

**The Handbook of Art Therapy and Digital Technology**
*Edited by Cathy Malchiodi, PhD*
*Foreword by Dr Val Huet*
ISBN 978 1 78592 792 8
eISBN 978 1 78450 774 9

**Art Therapy with Older Adults**
**Connected and Empowered**
*Erin Partridge*
ISBN 978 1 78592 824 6
eISBN 978 1 78450 940 8

**Art Therapy, Race and Culture**
*Edited by Jean Campbell, Marian Liebmann, Frederica*
*Brooks, Jenny Jones and Cathy Ward*
ISBN 978 1 85302 578 5
eISBN 978 0 85700 234 1

**Using Art Therapy with Diverse Populations**
**Crossing Cultures and Abilities**
*Paula Howie, Sangeeta Prasad and Jennie Kristel*
*Foreword by Mercedes B. ter Maat and Gaelynn P. Wolf Bordonaro*
ISBN 978 1 84905 916 9
eISBN 978 0 85700 694 3

**Art Therapy in Asia**
**To the Bone or Wrapped in Silk**
*Edited by Debra Kalmanowitz, Jordan S. Potash and Siu Mei Chan*
ISBN 978 1 84905 210 8
eISBN 978 0 85700 449 9

# CULTURAL HUMILITY IN ART THERAPY

Applications for Practice, Research,
Social Justice, Self-Care, and Pedagogy

Louvenia C. Jackson,
PhD, MFT, ATR-BC

*Foreword by Dr. Melanie Tervalon*

**Jessica Kingsley Publishers**
London and Philadelphia

First published in 2020
by Jessica Kingsley Publishers
73 Collier Street
London N1 9BE, UK
and
400 Market Street, Suite 400
Philadelphia, PA 19106, USA

*www.jkp.com*

**Library of Congress Cataloging in Publication Data**
A CIP catalog record for this book is available from the Library of Congress

**British Library Cataloguing in Publication Data**
A CIP catalogue record for this book is available from the British Library

ISBN 978 1 78592 643 3
eISBN 978 1 78592 644 0

Printed and bound in the United States

*This body of writing is dedicated to the phenomenal Black women that raised me to believe that I could reach my dreams and accomplish whatever goals I set in front of me with trust in God, faith, grace, and humility; my mother, Linda S. Redd, and my grandmother, Katherine James. Mom without your unconditional love, support, and sacrifice I could not have made it this far. Love you more than these words could express.*

# Contents

# Foreword

January 28, 2019, 8:00 am

This crisp, cool, clear morning I'm happily perched on the balcony lounge chair outside of my suite at Pueblo Bonito Emerald Bay, Mazatlán. The long stretch of ocean view is dramatic, with the pale white blue edge of the sky meeting the ocean's navy blue depths, creating the precise demarcation of the horizon. Nature in all of her glory makes breath-taking art at every turn of the eye in this place of beauty.

It was here in Mazatlán that I came to relax and paint in January of 2016, feeling extremely fatigued and certain that I only needed to rest, without the demands of a daily schedule and the pressures of work. I painted several beautiful pieces then, often from the bed, because I was just that tired.

I returned home to an urgent call from my primary care doctor, informing me that something was terribly wrong in the results from the routine blood work that was drawn the day before I left for my trip away. Within a month, I was diagnosed with multiple myeloma, a blood cancer, whose eradication requires a demanding chemotherapeutic regimen followed by a cutting edge and dramatic autologous stem cell transplant. I've been through this full course of treatment and now, in 2019, I'm in remission. I give thanks to so many, in so many ways.

And I give a special kind of thanks to the medium of watercolor and all the art in the world. Already in Mazatlán, during that 2016 visit, my body and soul were calling me to paint as a way to slow down and calm down and open my being up to some ease and healing. Once the diagnosis became clear, my urge to paint arrived with regularity. On days when I couldn't find the strength to step out from the bed or sit up for any length of time, my sister would bring a wooden food tray, my paints, paper, brushes, and plastic containers filled with water to the bed. There I lost myself in the glory of blue hues I placed on paper, or greens or reds, and in the process produced a series called: "Colors of the Cavern of the Unknown." The pieces cover the trajectory of my unwritten and unspoken inner life in color, through the transplant procedure from preparation through recovery. I also painted a single lined portrait from my bed, the night before the transplant began, which I have hanging in my bedroom as a reminder of my body in that moment, so frail, so undone.

Painting guided me during those months that turned into years into the sub-layers of my unsettled soul. There were no words when I painted, and, often, no sense of time or thought. Only the paints and paper, the brush strokes and the remarkable results. My spirit changed with painting. My being felt brushed free of worry. And, for those hours, the cancer left the center of the stage and, instead, colors and magic danced before my eyes, penetrating my soul and lifting me into the possibility of being well again. For me, painting is one form of ongoing self-reflection and lifelong learning that unveils the complexity of the interior architecture of my life, as my life unfolds, again and again in the face of each new day.

This book introduces us to the experience of art as an exploration and discovery of applying the framework and principles of cultural humility, in the context of the most critical issues of our world – justice, equity, and the creation of peace. Jann Murray Garcia and I, co-authors of the concept of cultural humility, thank the authors for their originality and imagination in organizing and presenting this work into the field of art therapy and look forward to the healing that arrives with its publication.

With love, gratitude and in peace,

Dr. Melanie Tervalon

# Acknowledgments

With sincere gratitude, I would like to express recognition to the following individuals and communities that supported my journey in completing this manuscript. I would not be the human being I am today without the unconditional love and encouragement of the phenomenally strong women of my family. I hold in high regard the care and compassion of my eldest brother and his children. This book would not be possible without the efforts, advocacy, humility, and determination of Dr. Jann Murray-Garcia and Dr. Melanie Tervalon. Thanks to Dr. Erin Partridge for editing and to Dr. Melanie Tervalon for her cover art. The warmest regards go to the fantastic Black women who collaborated, saw possibility and importance to engage in the collective research study that offered the foundations to examining cultural humility in art therapy. Thank you to all that contributed their reflections, artwork, and images to this manuscript. I have been honored and blessed with the knowledge, support, and commitment of the faculty in the Art Therapy Psychology Department at Notre Dame de Namur University and the Martial and Family Therapy Department with the Specialization in Art Therapy at Loyola Marymount University. And to Morris Brown College, the HBCU that help me solidify my identity as an educated, creative, Black woman. To my family, friends, neighbors, and communities: without your support and encouragement I would not have had the confidence and light to walk this path. A special note of appreciation goes to the students, colleagues, and individuals who I have been blessed to come in contact with and learn from. And to the art therapists who have prompted and advocated for the topic of cultural equity within art therapy, your work, foundation, courage, and activism to change the perspectives and practices in the field, gave me a path in which to walk and learn from. Much love to all of you.

# CHAPTER 1

# Integration of Cultural Humility in Art Therapy

## Cultural humility echoed in art therapy history

Cultural awareness, diversity, and competence have been discussed in art therapy since the beginnings of the practice. Individuals such as Lucile Venture wrote about the need for diversity within the field of art therapy and its approaches (Venture, 1977). Other early pioneers of color such as Georgette Seabrook Powell and Sarah McGee would continue to contribute and display accountability in this area (Gipson, 2019). From there, many early art therapists went on to echo the need (Boston & Short, 1998; Campbell *et al.*, 1999; Gerity, 2000; Henley, 1999; Hiscox & Calisch, 1998; Hocoy, 2002; Huss, 2009; McGann, 2006; McNiff, 2009; Talwar, Iyer, & Doby-Copeland, 2004). In recent years, many other art therapists have continued the conversation through critical lenses (Awais & Yali, 2013; Dye, 2017; Gipson, 2015; Jackson, Mezzera, & Satterberg, 2018; Karcher, 2017; Kuri, 2017; Potash *et al.*, 2015, 2017; Potash & Ramirez, 2013; Talwar, 2015, 2017; ter Maat, 2011). It is well known that statistics suggest art therapists aren't very ethnically diverse and for many years there has been a desire for cultural approaches that are inclusive of the individuals that engage in art therapy practices. Upon entering the field, I was encouraged to apply to the Master's program in Marital and Family Therapy (MFT)/ Art Therapy because it was stated that "you're needed," referring to me being a woman of color. As I entered classes surrounded by mostly identified white females and white professors, it was evident to me that cultural representation other than the dominant culture was needed. I sought out art therapists of color near my location and searched for diversity and cultural relevance in art therapy literature.

There have been numerous articles in the American Art Therapy Association's (AATA) *Art Therapy Journal* that feature accounts from art therapists of color. Of particular interest is the series "Stories of Art Therapists of Color," in which contributors (such as Boston, 2005; Boston & Short, 2006; Doby-Copeland, 2006b; Farris, 2006; Hocoy, 2006; Joseph, 2006; Levy, 2006; Lumpkin, 2006; Potash, 2005) bravely and candidly reflect on self-identity and the practice of art therapy through a cultural lens. There are also books such as Hiscox and Calisch's (1998) *Tapestry of Cultural Issues in Art Therapy*, which offer reflections on cultural sensitivity and awareness. Other books and articles have focused on specific populations, expanding the many publications that have included the conversation of cultural awareness and cultural competence (Campbell *et al.*, 1999; Dokter, 1998; Forrest-Bank *et al.*, 2016; Hanania, 2018; Huss, 2018; Kalmanowitz & Ho, 2016; Kerr, 2015; Liebmann & Weston, 2015; Maat, 1997; McNiff, 2009; Park, 2017; Partridge, 2019; Potash, Chan, & Kalmanowitz, 2012; Slayton, 2012; Weinberg, 2018).

The AATA's *Art Therapy Journal* published a special issue on culture, diversity, and identity in 2015 (Talwar, 2015), which offered important reflections on cultural aspects of art therapy. It provided details of the history and development of the AATA Multicultural Committee and its impact on the field with regard to cultural awareness. Many prominent individuals of color in the field of art therapy were contributors to this essential issue, which covered topics of social justice, increasing diversity in the field of art therapy, and cultural competence in pedagogy. The timely distribution of this issue spoke to the need and interest in this topic area.

Although all these publications are extremely important and relevant, the introduction of cultural humility in art therapy was absent until the unpublished graduate projects by Har-Gil (2010) and then my own doctoral work (Jackson, 2016). The practice of cultural humility itself has been documented for many years since its inception in 1998. Most have integrated it in the practice of medicine, education, nursing, clinical psychology, counseling, psychiatry, public administration, and social work (Abdul-Raheem, 2018; Andrews, Kim, & Watanabe, 2018; Danso, 2018; Hook *et al.*, 2016; Lopez-Littleton & Burr, 2018; Loue, 2018; Tisdell *et al.*, 2019;

Yeung *et al.*, 2018). Recently, cultural humility and art therapy have been included in journal publications (Bal & Kaur, 2018; Keselman & Awais, 2018).

## The impact of multiculturalism

Although a new approach and philosophy, cultural humility was met by some with hesitation, as the term humility brought about comparisons to competence. Some felt as if moving away from the term cultural competence would dismiss or devalue the work that had been done by previous art therapy pioneers and advocates who sought to shift the importance of competence within art therapy. It was urged that, before focusing on humility, cultural competence in art therapy and the associated work should be studied, honored, and illuminated. While this remains imperative and relevant, when examined, both humility and competence in cultural approaches within the field of art therapy are needed. There is a place for both amongst the conversation of inclusion, diversity, and equity. Cultural competence gave language and tangible practices sought for at that time. But, with cultural competence, there was an area missing within many training models, which required catapulting further from the named skills of the practice to more expansive ways of applying cultural awareness on a deeper level.

According to Sue and Sue (1999), becoming a multicultural competent mental health practitioner involves three dimensions. The first dimension relates to the practitioner's attitudes and beliefs about race, culture, ethnicity, gender, sexual orientation; personal biases and the need to monitor them, and how those values and biases can affect therapy. The second is knowledge and understanding of one's worldview, possessing specific knowledge of the diverse group with whom they work, and having a basic understanding of sociopolitical influences. The third deals with skills, intervention techniques, and strategies necessary for serving diverse client groups.

Sue and Sue (1999) were convinced that the field of clinical and counseling psychology had failed to meet the particular mental health needs of ethnic minorities. They suggested that the reasons half of the minority clients that come to counseling terminate or seek other services are due to the nature of the services themselves (cited in Corey, Corey, & Callanan, 2003). Over the years, multicultural issues have been addressed from many different angles. Sue and Sue help build a foundation through the development of multicultural competencies. Although some questions have been raised about these competencies (Arredondo, 1999), multicultural competencies have served as a specific outline that integrates issues of diversity into a practitioner's interaction with racial and ethnic minorities.

At the time when cultural competence was being introduced and integrated into practice, ethics codes in multicultural counseling were also put in place. Four governing bodies were examined in a review of how their ethnic codes were implemented and stated. During the late 1990s and early 2000s there were changes in ethics codes across the mental health spectrum. The code of ethics of the American Counseling Association (ACA) (1995) called for members to recognize diversity in our society and embrace a cross-cultural approach in support of the worth, dignity, potential, and uniqueness of each individual (cited in Corey *et al.*, 2003). The American Psychological Association (APA) ethics code (1992) indicated that differences of age, gender, race, ethnicity, national origin, religion, sexual orientation, disability, language, or socioeconomic status significantly affect psychologists' work concerning particular individuals or groups; psychologists obtain the training, experience, consultation, or supervision necessary to ensure the competence of their services, or they make appropriate referrals (cited in Corey *et al.*, 2003). Focusing on one state's standards as an example, the California Association of Marriage and Family Therapists' (CAMFT) (2004) ethical standards on Professional Competence and Integrity (3.6) stated that:

> Marriage and family therapists actively strive to understand the diverse cultural backgrounds of their clients by gaining knowledge, personal awareness, and developing sensitivity and skills pertinent to working with a diverse client population. Marriage and family therapists who provide therapy over the Internet or by other electronic media take extra measures to identify and understand the diversity, ethnicity, and cultural sensitivity of such patients.

Ethical standard (3.7) states, "Marriage and family therapists are aware of how their cultural/racial/ethnic identity, values, and beliefs affect the process of therapy."

American Art Therapy Association (AATA) (2004) ethical standards for art therapists, (6.0) Multicultural Competence, defined cultural competence as:

> A set of congruent behaviors, attitudes, and policies that enable art therapists to work effectively in cross-cultural situations. Art therapists acknowledge and incorporate into their professional work the importance of culture; variations within cultures; the assessment of cross-cultural relations; cultural differences in visual symbols and imagery; vigilance towards the dynamics that result from cultural differences; the expansion of cultural knowledge; and the adaptation of services to meet culturally-unique needs.

The Multicultural Competence goes on to list six specific guidelines to address cultural competence amongst art therapists (6.1–6.6).

Efforts have recently been made to go beyond these ethical standards to be more inclusive and direct. In the 2014 ACA code of ethics, a reference to cultural competence was placed in every section. As it applies to the counseling relationship, Section A includes A.2.c., addressing Developmental and Cultural Sensitivity. Section B, Confidentiality and Privacy, states, "Counselors maintain awareness and sensitivity regarding cultural meanings of confidentiality and privacy." From there it goes on to include a non-discrimination clause in the Professional Accountability section, a cultural sensitivity clause in Evaluation, Assessment and Interpretation, a multicultural issues/diversity clause in Supervision, infusing multicultural issues/diversity in educational, student diversity, multicultural/ diversity competence in Counselor Education and Training Programs, as well as multicultural and disability considerations in Distance Counseling, Technology, and Social Media (American Counseling Association, 2014).

With reported years of amendments, the APA's Ethical Principles of Psychologists and Code of Conduct begins with the principles of "Justice" and "Respect for People's Rights and Dignity." Besides these principles, no other sections of the document speak specifically to diversity (American Psychological Association, 2017).

The CAMFT code of ethics, revised in 2011, first standard refers to the "Responsibility to the Patient":

NON-DISCRIMINATION: Marriage and family therapists do not condone or engage in discrimination, or refuse professional service to anyone on the basis of race, gender, gender identity, gender expression, religion, national origin, age, sexual orientation, disability, socioeconomic, or marital status. Marriage and family therapists make reasonable efforts to accommodate patients who have physical disabilities.

Later, in Section 3, Professional Competence and Integrity, Section 3.6 states, "CULTURAL SENSITIVITY: Marriage and family therapists actively strive to identify and understand the diverse cultural backgrounds of their clients by gaining knowledge, personal awareness, and developing sensitivity and skills pertinent to working with a diverse client population." In relation to supervisor, student, and supervisee responsibilities, it states, "CULTURAL DIVERSITY: Supervisors and educators are aware of and address the role that culture and diversity issues play in the supervisory relationship, including, but not limited to, evaluating, terminating, disciplining, or making decisions regarding supervisees or students."

The AATA's *Ethical Principles for Art Therapists*, revised in 2013, begins with Justice as one of its values, with a blanket statement, "Art therapists commit to treating all persons with fairness. Art therapists ensure that clients have equal access to services." Within the document Section 7 is dedicated to Multicultural and Diversity Competency, with seven codes addressing non-discrimination practices, sensitivity to differences, awareness of one's own values and beliefs, obtaining education on social diversity and oppression, acquiring knowledge and information about specific cultural groups, culturally sensitive education and supervision, and the guidance of the association's Multicultural and Diversity Competencies. These ethics standards brought forth an understanding that recognizing cultural diversity within the practice of mental health is one of importance and inclusion. Although stated differently across disciplines the significance is pungently indicated. The ACA includes diversity in every ethical consideration and code. It does not stand outside of practice but integrated within. CAMFT has made more efforts in recent years to include diversity in other codes as well as to create a code for cultural sensitivity. And both the APA and AATA have made little effort to directly incorporate cultural diversity into the language of their ethics codes. Overall, they have both made blanket statements and generalized some codes throughout. The changes and evolution of each practice convey whether cultural diversity is seen as being integrated into practice or an aspect of practice. This book hopes to make it apparent that cultural diversity considerations and applications need to be an inclusive and integrated mindset, with principles designed to be a way of knowing in the practice of cultural humility within art therapy.

## Defining cultural humility in art therapy

Cultural humility is derived of a set of principles that offer grounding for cultural awareness. It is a skill set and a state of being that can offer a way to engage in critical cultural discourse. It is not a one-size-fits-all and may be difficult for some to absorb and cultivate. It is a way of developing a worldview with integrity and respect for oneself and those one works with. It can bring dignity to those who have felt stripped of their sense of self as well as lending empowerment to those whose voices have been denied witnessing. It offers a tangible way to enter into dialogue when tensions are surmounting all sense of reason and hope.

My concentration on cultural humility was sparked because "it fit with my worldview and who I am as an individual…as it reflected my own journey and story" (Gallardo, 2014, p.3). After focusing on multiculturalism in art therapy for my thesis work, I went into the field to practice and felt that there were minimal conversations happening about how providers' worldviews impacted their practice. I witnessed this in many areas from different health providers I worked alongside. There appeared to be avoidance in acknowledging these biases, assumptions, and beliefs and more of a focus on understanding what was perceived as the other. Cultural humility spoke to that missing piece of self-reflection and accountability. It offered a way of acknowledging the lack of insight without blaming while encouraging activation in the spaces where awareness was missing. After more investigation into the concept, I became aware of the importance of cultural humility in that it "captures a value that I think needs to be incorporated in our multicultural discussion" (Gallardo, 2014, p.3); I became interested in how it could be specifically applied to art therapy practice, research, and theory.

I was first introduced to cultural humility while attending a training academy in 2007 for chairs of newly developed initiatives, which was constructed through the Office of Diversity and Equity (ODE) at San Mateo County. These initiatives were made up of diverse cultural groups that composed the populations within the county. They included African American, Pacific Islander, Latino, Chinese, and LGBTQIA, to name a few. In the final graduating class, the group received a special presentation from Dr. Melanie Tervalon, who introduced the concept of cultural humility. By the end of the day, she had guided and facilitated the chairs of the initiatives into discussing our frustrations and creating an action plan of next steps for getting those needs addressed. This included an active listening of our lived experiences from our different cultural backgrounds, an action plan, and a list of accountabilities to that action plan for those chairs present in the room. We felt heard, validated, and inspired. From that point on, I embarked on a journey in social advocacy utilizing the concepts of cultural humility. I began with digital media, which was encouraged by those administrators who had brought the digital media platform to the county in which I participated in, and then brought to the population I was practicing with.

This introduction to creative practice and cultural humility expanded as I engaged in presentations, conference workshops, and educational implementations through lecture and assessment. I began practicing the principles and sharing them with others in the art therapy field. I believed that the principles of cultural humility integrated seamlessly with the practice and theories of art therapy.

Although developed for physicians and the medical field, cultural humility speaks to the humanness in many disciplines that provide health services to individuals and communities.

Tervalon and Murray-Garcia (1998) developed a multicultural curriculum project described in their article, "Cultural humility versus cultural competence: a critical distinction in defining physician training outcomes in multicultural education." This was sparked by a statement made by a colleague who expressed that "cultural competence in practice is best defined not by a discreet endpoint, but a commitment and active engagement in a lifelong process that individuals enter into on an ongoing basis with patients, communities, colleagues, and with themselves" (Tervalon & Murray-Garcia, 1998, p.118). Tervalon and Murray-Garcia described the components of cultural humility as follows:

- "Cultural humility is a lifelong process of self-reflection and self-critique whereby the individual not only learns about another's culture, but one starts with an examination of… [one's] own beliefs and cultural identities" (as cited in Yeager & Bauer-Wu, 2013, para. 5).

- Cultural humility "address[es] the power imbalance and sees the individual or community as rich experts, teachers on the content of culture" (as cited in Africa & Endres, 2009, p.31).

- Cultural humility "recognizes the dynamic nature of culture since cultural influences change over time and vary depending on location" (as cited in Yeager & Bauer-Wu, 2013, para. 5).

- Cultural humility is "not a discrete end point but, a commitment and active engagement in a lifelong process that individuals enter into on an ongoing basis with patients, communities, colleagues, and with themselves" (Tervalon & Murray-Garcia, 1998, p.118).

Cultural humility is a way to be inclusive of other ways of knowing outside the Western paradigm, which art therapy was founded on; it conveys the importance of recognizing that the foci of expertise with regard to health can indeed reside outside of the academic medical center and even outside of the practice of Western medicine (Tervalon & Murray-Garcia, 1998). When investigating art therapy institutions, Tervalon and Murray-Garcia (1998) conveyed the importance of self-reflection and self-critique at the institutional level. Given AATA's statistics on the overwhelming number of white female members as reflections of practitioners in the field, using cultural humility to investigate this dynamic is relevant. Tervalon and Murray-Garcia (1998) charged that self-reflection and critique need to encompass "honest, thorough, and ongoing responses" to questions such as "what is the demographic profile…is the composition inclusive of members of diverse cultural racial, ethnic, and sexual orientation backgrounds?" (p.122).

---

## The four cultural humility principles

* A lifelong process of critical self-reflection and self-critique.

* Readdressing the power imbalance in the patient–provider dynamic.

* Developing mutually beneficial partnerships with communities on behalf of and defined populations.

* Advocating for and maintaining institutional accountability. (Tervalon & Lewis, 2018)

---

In other words, Tervalon and Murray-Garcia (1998) put forth the challenge to researchers to capture "the characteristics of cultural humility in individuals and institutions" (p.122). They advocated doing this through the use of "mixed methodologies that use qualitative methods (including participants' observations, key informant interviews, journals, and mechanisms for community feedback) and action research models to complement traditional quantitative assessment" (p.122). Using creativity in both developing and evaluating programs "will help avoid the pitfall of adopting the status quo in documenting clinical competence" (p.122). This will be addressed specifically and integrated with the above principles throughout this book to offer a way of using cultural humility in art therapy practice, education, and research. Applied effectively, cultural humility research and theory can assist in the balance of art therapy practice.

One must strike a delicate balance when addressing cultural humility through art. Art therapists are challenged to not allow themselves to become intellectually arrogant. Most art therapists have an understanding of art as the limitless use of their imagination to depict their reality, and that they have the wisdom to understand art's capabilities. This can place art therapists in the role of power and privilege over those they work with. The task for art therapists is to hold their knowledge without becoming arrogant when working with clients. Cultural humility offers a possible solution, as "humility appears to be very important to clients when addressing their cultural worldview" (Hook *et al.*, 2013, p.361). After measuring openness to culturally diverse clients using cultural humility, Hook *et al.* (2013) expressed that "engaging a culturally diverse client with an interpersonal stance of humility may attenuate the tendency for therapists to overvalue their own perspectives and worldviews, instead of joining with the client to explore the client's perspective and worldview" (p.361). This relates to the importance of self-reflection in cultural humility and using it as an ongoing practice as a way to not do harm; instead, in practice with awareness an art therapist can flourish in cultural humility, empowering their clients.

The premise of the self-reflection asked of practitioners is developed through the concept of developing cultural humility through art. Self-reflection in cultural humility encourages a person to know who they are, including one's history, experience, and worldview (Tervalon, 2015). Cultural humility asks for one to engage in honest self-reflection about one's social and cultural identity (Tervalon, 2015). This can be relevant and achieved in numerous ways to alleviate possible suffering in the field of art therapy, and for those whom art therapists serve. One of the ways this can be done is through response art (Fish, 2012; Lavery, 1994). After working with a client, group, or population, difficult feelings can arise. Although response art has been done for many years by art therapists as a way to process difficult emotions and reactions, the ethnic, racial, sexual, gender, religious, regional, language, and so on, considerations and impacts that occur in interactions with clients should be included in the exploration of transference and countertransference; deeply investigating the art therapist's assumptions, biases, and beliefs is the essential goal. Reflective art can assist the art therapist in working through challenging interactions with clients. It can allow the therapist to acknowledge countertransference and consultation (Tervalon, 2015). At the end of every chapter in this book an exercise to stimulate self-reflection will be offered, along with responsive reflections and response art from those practicing and advocating cultural humility in art therapy. The hope is that when reading these reflections and viewing the response art, the therapist will be inspired and illuminated as to how cultural humility can impact art therapy in areas of research, practice, community-based work, social advocacy, introspection, and pedagogy. The responsive reflections, which are offered by different individuals at the end of each chapter, and in different formats, are incorporated to act as a model and a mirror for the reader's engagement in self-reflection.

The aspect of self-reflection through art can also increase cultural humility if done on an ongoing basis. If an art therapist is not participating in art as a continuous practice, he or she can be removed from the significance and ramifications of engaging in self-reflection with the tools of the profession (British Association of Art Therapists [BAAT], 2014). If a therapist is unaware of what can emerge from an art directive before giving it to a client, they may not be aware of how that client may react by doing that directive, and this can cause clients to engage in therapeutic practices with art in ways that can be damaging. Springham (2008) spoke about art being "real" and said "people regularly have strong visceral reactions to art, as if something beyond the material object itself is real" (p.70). This conveys the importance of art therapy education and an art therapist's ongoing art practice, as individuals may have responses to the art that a non-practicing art therapist is not trained and/or attuned to mediate.

Through continuous art practice, an art therapist can develop stronger empathy, awareness, and congruence. This practice may include the creative practice of exploring different art mediums, writing, and movement from diverse cultural aspects and populations. A key component of cultural humility is self-reflection and a lifelong inquiry in understanding those we serve and work with. Using art reflection can assist the art therapist in working through countertransference that may block the flow of trust between client and art therapist. It can also help the art therapist to have a clearer understanding of themselves in order to communicate more effectively with diverse populations. This aligns with the AATA's ethical practices.

One rationale for adhering to ethical standards is to build trust in the quality and integrity of the program (Elsayed & Ahmed, 2009). Ethical practices for the profession are promoted when the public is aware that art therapists are dedicated to practicing art therapy themselves through the continuous practice of art. These practices may lead to a more integrated approach to art therapy that involves the collaboration of practice, not simply the practice of a top-down approach. Being culturally humble may require one to move away from leading from the front and alternatively to be with the client as a way of empowerment and adjusting the power imbalance that can occur in art therapy.

Cultural humility supports a step away from the etic pedagogy to one that is emic. Unlike cultural competence, cultural humility is interconnected with truth, gives power to each voice, is personal, authentic, organic, mutually developed, and skill based. It includes dialogue, reflection, and ongoing, fluid, engagement. It allows all those involved to be the learner and student. It is teachable, encompasses partnership, shared decision-making, and is flexible and dynamic (Tervalon, 2015).

It is important for an art therapist to have good communication, trust, accountability, mutual respect, and fair medical care (Elsayed & Ahmed, 2009). Tervalon and Murray-Garcia (1998) state that practitioners need to listen to the patient in a "less authoritative style that signals to the patient that the practitioner values what the patient's agenda and perspectives are, both biomedical and nonbiomedical" (p.121). Hook *et al.* (2013) suggested the importance of "interpersonal behaviors such as expressions of humility" (p.362), and then offered examples such as "being open to explore the client's cultural background, asking questions when uncertain, expressing curiosity and interest about the client's cultural worldview" (p.362). The practice of respectful, curious inquiry follows the idea that curiosity sparks creativity. An art therapist who is open to inquiry before analyzing and diagnosing will allow space for creativity to flourish between the client, the art therapist, and the art. Recognizing the art therapist as the student, partner, and facilitator with access to resources and knowledge can create a holding environment where art therapy practice becomes an integrated experience. Being open to other ways of knowing through art can allow for the individual or community to be viewed as rich experts and teachers on the context of their culture, avoiding the "isms" that cause stress in community life. Avoiding the checklist of "cultural traits" can be achieved by being present with clients and illuminating collective learning. Relating to one's human connectedness can encourage, rather than obstruct, the telling of the story. Cultural humility involves learning to listen to the stories of one's clients, not only using one's ears, eyes, and undivided attention, as art therapists have been trained to do, but, most importantly, it involves listening with one's heart. Many of the above-mentioned statements regarding self-reflection, ways of knowing and practicing, and others will be further elaborated upon and explored throughout this book.

In this body of work, each chapter will focus on characteristics of cultural humility needed in art therapy practice. Included are Chapter 2, Research and Assessment, which examines the "body" or whole person; Chapter 3, Art Therapy Practice that uses "eyes" to explore worldview in facilitation; Chapter 4, Community-Based Art Therapy and the use of "hands" to reach out and connect; Chapter 5, Approaches to Social Justice while reverberating compassion and a brave "heart" for advocacy; Chapter 6, Introspection and Self-Care by flowing through the "circular" patterns of the humanity in humility; and Chapter 7, Pedagogy and the "symbols" that we use to develop meaning. Each of these characteristics (body, eyes, hands, heart, circle, symbols) was extracted by the words and art of the Black women art therapists who engaged in my dissertation research, titled "Acquiring new knowledge through art self-exploration and collective journaling to enhance cultural humility in art therapy" (Jackson, 2016), which will be discussed in the next chapter.

## REFLECTIVE PERSPECTIVE

My focus on culture using art has been almost lifelong. One of my earliest recollections is running for eighth-grade class president, where I used my artistic skills to depict hand-drawn images on my campaign posters. Later, I was elected and offered a speech to my school on the importance of recognizing others' strengths to help to achieve a common goal. In high school, I used dance, art, and playwriting to express the concerns of my cultural group. In earning my Bachelor's in Fine Art at Morris Brown College, I discovered self-reflection through the art, life, and work of Frida Kahlo. I continued to create self-portraits, something I had begun to do during high school; I developed this work into a series, which comprised my final display of work. I depicted myself similarly to selected works of Frida Kahlo. I did not have the psychological framework, but I was working through identification in these self-images. At the same time, I was keeping a journal, reflecting on the challenges I was facing in developing into a Black woman. It was in my Master's program at Notre Dame de Namur University (NDNU) that my passion for culture, self-reflection, and art became cohesive. Through my art therapy education, I developed a workshop, "Rediscover a new way of understanding human behavior and cultural diversity through self-examination: increase self-knowledge and deepen your understanding of others and the universe," which evolved into my thesis, the "Circle of culture: enhancing multicultural and self-awareness through implementing optimal psychology to art therapy with art therapy graduate students." I was not aware of cultural humility at that time, but later I learned about it through my work as a creative arts therapist for San Mateo County, and I soon realized that it was the key to tying my passion and life's work together. After being introduced to cultural humility, I embarked on a journey in social advocacy, along with utilizing the concepts of cultural humility with digital media. The ODE at the county began a series of digital storytelling projects. I was privileged to be a part of most of these. The projects were designed to support the values of ODE, which were cultural competence and cultural humility, shared and multicultural leadership, building bridges and sustainability of partnerships, forward and out of the box thinking, advocacy, and community capacity, and the use of data to determine outcomes. I was asked to compile all the projects into a presentation. After developing a PowerPoint presentation, I began presenting these digital story-telling projects (Stories with Heart), without yet truly grasping the concept of cultural humility. Upon entering the Art Therapy PhD program at NDNU, through my doctoral research, I began to further educate myself on the concept of cultural humility.

"The combination of individual experience with cultural experience is crucial in the process phase of autoethnography, as the personal perception shapes the way that a particular culture is viewed" (LaFrance & Blizzard, 2013, p.26). As a Black woman, culture is relevant in all areas of my life. As an artist, I have always found ways to express my experience of being a Black female through creative means. Art was the way I developed an understanding of the world, and art was how I wrote journals, poetry, plays, and speeches. During my undergraduate degree in fine art, I discovered painting. This medium offered a flow that I had needed to engage in the self-reflective process. The art I was creating before then was very methodical and with structured materials. Painting gave me the art form to freely express from a place other than my mind construct. I was able to create from within, developing a way of understanding myself. Art not only allowed me to communicate and understand my own thoughts and feelings, I also became aware of the thoughts and feelings of others through their responses to the art I was creating. It was not until I discovered art therapy that I began to understand the importance of art to social and cultural experience.

I was enlightened and intrigued in my undergraduate program by the artist Frida Kahlo. The strength and personal insight she displayed in her artwork astounded me. Her work inspired me to begin a series of self-portraits, many of which were fashioned after some of Kahlo's works of art. I had no psychological verbiage or understanding for what I was doing, but there was healing and comfort in being able to reflect myself in these creative images. Looking for identity and deciphering "Art is Life," wrote DeLuca

(2015), in a recent article in *Essence Magazine*. I resonated with the words of the editor right away, particularly when she addressed the "transformative power of the arts" (p.14). I recalled my own experiences with the arts and how they had manifested change in my life. The editor concluded the article by stating, "Creative expression is a cultural lifeline" (p.14). I find this to be true in so many ways. Creativity integrates the parts of us into complete and whole human beings; it heals us from within and without. Our soul would wither away without it (DeLuca, 2015). In one of the article's final sentences, a word that has been debated by others who have read my dissertation had particular resonance for me. DeLuca encouraged others to "tap into the *innate* spirit to make art that lives inside each of us" (p.14). Natural, intrinsic, instinctive, intuitive art expression and healing—this I believe is a power within all of us. We all carry within us an innate spirit or wisdom to create art as a way of understanding, and it is through this practice that we can integrate our whole being. Understanding this innate engagement with the art is how I believe cultural humility relates to art therapy. It is intuitive if allowed to approach the art without the oppression of others, to engage in the art as a way of healing holistically. Often, when not culturally humble, an art therapist can interrupt the intrinsic flow of the art expression, not allowing the artist to convey the wisdom they hold within. It was not until recent years that I also began to appreciate the cultural significance of Frida Kahlo's artwork. It has been noted that an important facet of her work is its sensitivity to a specifically Mexican tradition (Milner, 2004). Kahlo's work exudes a potent mixture of personal history, cultural inheritance, political commitment, and sheer self-conscious myth-making. Frida used art as a way of knowing that was not tied to Western philosophy. Her art reflected her own personal experiences as well as the cultural and societal influences that were intertwined in her innate creative expressions. It is through the journey of self-knowledge and cultural self-identity that one obtains wisdom. The idea that "wisdom comes from self-understanding" (Martin & Barresi, 2006, p.11) is derived from the reflections of Heraclitus. Wisdom is the acknowledgment of our lived experience (Jackson, 2016, pp.2–4).

## RESPONSE ART

*Figure 1.1 Self-portrait collage by Louvenia C. Jackson, 2019*

## REFLECTIVE EXERCISE A: **SELF-PORTRAIT**

■ **Goal:** Explore the aspects of self through creative medium.

The first step to self-exploration and the understanding of others is to first explore your understanding/meaning of self. Creating self-portraits can bring awareness to the true self, which Winnicott (1960) defined as the part that is creative, spontaneous, and real (Jackson, 2016, p.123). The self-reflective process of cultural humility enacted through a self-portrait illuminates the important first step of placing one's self in a cultural context.

■ **Materials:** Structured materials (novice): paper, pencil, markers, crayons, color pencils, collage (cut paper and glue). Expressive materials (experienced): paint, watercolor, wet clay, pastels.

■ **Prompt:** Spend a significant amount of time examining yourself in a mirror. Pay attention to biases, assumptions, and beliefs being projected. Allow the thoughts to be acknowledged then pass, while moving on to different area or part of your reflection. If helpful, jot down those thoughts and feelings. While exploring aesthetics, which may also lead to judgments, focus on the formal elements and structure.

When ready, place the mirror in front of you, allowing your visual form to be in your line of sight while creating your reflection. Periodically, look into the mirror and back at your artwork, again taking note of thoughts, feelings, or behaviors that may arise.

Create until the portrait feels complete; this may take 5–10 minutes or a few hours. Make an effort to be as spontaneous as possible, allowing for creative expression that derives from a genuine place. The idea is to move away from perfection or realistic representation and flow into an open space of honoring whatever depiction is created.

After the reflection is created, sit for a moment allowing for latent content to arise. Address the obvious and search for the hidden. Again, write down the things you find significant and relevant to cultural meaning. This may be size, use of color, focal point, perception of space and time, familiarity, and so on. These and other factors will be elaborated on in the next exercise. As cultural humility is a lifelong process, this self-portrait maybe one of many that you create as you continue to examine your relation to self and other.

# CHAPTER 2

# Cultural Humility in Art Therapy Research and Assessment

*Body (Figure, Form): The Whole Person, Intersectionality and Inclusion*

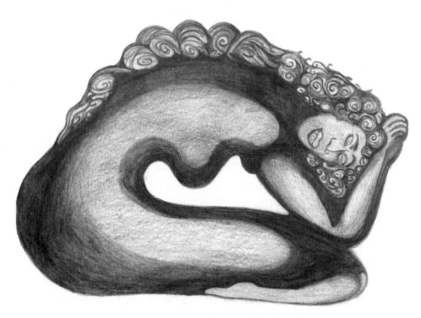

*Figure 2.1 Female figure in fetal position, Collective Study Collaborator Art 011*

## Western influence on ways of knowing

It has been stated by many art therapists that the field and practice of art therapy have been rooted in Western psychology. (Hocoy, 2002; Talwar, Iyer *et al.*, 2004). The field of art therapy has a strong scientific foundation, with limited influences or wisdom from other cultures and other ways of knowing. Robb (2012) stated, "Art therapy research began at NIH (National Institutes of Health) in 1958 with Hanna Kwiatkowska, whose work contributed to the foundation of art therapy with families, and with Harriet Wadeson, who conducted psychodynamic art therapy research" (p.33). In order to discuss the principles of cultural humility in art therapy assessment and research, the foundation of art therapy research must be examined. Cultural humility offers an alternative way of knowing which aligns more with non-Western philosophies, as it implies a non-linear processing, expansion in discovery, creation of meaning and exploration of multiple truths. Understanding Western philosophies and scientific knowing can illuminate a way of extrapolating to discover cultural humility in the realm of assessment and research.

Western philosophy is based on several principles such as scientific knowing, deductive reasoning, Truth (with big "T") (Martin & Barresi, 2006), Self (without interdependence), thinking styles such as linear, systematic observations, and analyses (Macleod, 1975). Western ideology, based on the scientific method, has marginalized ways of knowing that come from alternative thinking styles, such as myth and metaphor (Wildman & Inayatullah, 1996). Wildman and Inayatullah (1996) described "the Western 'scientific' type of mind" (p.729) as one that excludes other ways of thinking and knowing.

Current psychological theories and practices, which heavily influence art therapy, are based on scientific knowing. The scientific way of knowing has been, in turn, heavily influenced by men of the Enlightenment period, and their methods and theories still rein in today's science. Macleod (1975) stated, "The Newtonian system triumphed in the seventeenth century, dominated the sciences of the eighteenth and nineteenth centuries, set the pattern for the modern doctrine of man, and in the mid-twentieth century is still present in our implicit assumptions" (p.96). The scientific method seeks to gain knowledge through systematic observation. Newton's theory was that "as more and more facts are observed, recorded and analyzed, natural laws will be revealed that will completely explain the facts" (p.96). Newton and many other theorists of his time suggested that through observation, Truth could be proven (Macleod, 1975). Systematic observation is similar to the dehumanizing practices of colonization. It ignores the other aspects of being and the facts become defined by the dominant group that is engaging in the scientific research. This has been related to the practice of art therapy, where Hamrick and Byma (2017) convey, "Art therapists have called for the decolonization of art therapy (Gipson, 2015; Talwar, 2010, 2015), a field populated largely by white, heterosexual, cisgender women, and shaped by a medical discourse that is both Eurocentric and patriarchal (Talwar, Iyer, & Doby-Copeland, 2004)" (p.106). Later in the article, they

> identify the presence of racism in the profession of art therapy and provide a theoretical and historical basis for it. Although white people are the dominant group among professionals in the field… there is a lack of published research regarding the psychological conditions of white supremacy that shape it. (p.106)

This way of scientific approach to research continues to impact our way of knowing in art therapy.

With the development of systematic observation, science became about prediction and control. Knowledge was interpreted as cause and effect. Gergen (2000) noted that cause-and-effect relations among the elements are typically defined as knowledge. There were others who began to acknowledge, however, that matter was forever changing and that the Truth exists but can only be an approximation (Macleod, 1975). These new scientists began to view understanding as probability and hold that the whole of the Truth can never be known at one time (Macleod, 1975).

Systematic observation led to the cognitive way of knowing that has exerted an enormous influence on psychology. However, as Macleod (1975) suggested, the cognitive approach to knowledge can limit the understanding of truth: "Cognition is the process whereby we attain knowledge. Whether or not we can attain true knowledge is, as we have seen, one of the persistent problems of philosophy" (p.130). If Truth is not solely acquired through cognition and observation, then where does Truth lie? According to Dreikurs (1971) Truth is relative, "Truth and falsehood are relative to the situation" (p.171). Truth is conceptualized through the observer's point of view.

## Truth in art

One of the main concepts in cultural humility is allowing individuals and communities to define their own truth based on their lived experience. For the art therapist, it is important while being culturally humble to allow that same truth to be depicted in the art. This applies to research, assessment, and practice. Dissanayake (1995), reflecting on postmodernism philosophy and art as interpretation, suggested that truth or reality was only a representation of the individual. Truth is a perspective developed from one's language, social institutions, gender, class, profession, religious affiliations, and historical time frame. Dissanayake noted that artists have no special talent or privilege to the truth, but, like anyone else, interpret it according to "their individual and cultural sensibilities" (p.199).

Dissanayake (1995) cited Nietzsche in what was described as a severe thought, that "we have art in order to not perish of the truth," (p.91) a notion developed from Freudian psychology that somehow art is used to escape from uncomfortable aspects of our realities. Dissanayake stated that the necessity of art goes beyond self-expression. The notion of art as mere self-expression is derived from modern society, which views art as "superfluous, something decorative and enjoyable" (p.91). Dissanayake revealed that art is a "behavior," (p.10) not a product or a vessel for other behaviors, but one of our human traits in its own right

This reflective view is where the knowledge in art resides. Shottenkirk (2007) described art as both "dissent and truth" (p.4) and likened it to a brave voice similar to a shaman. Supported by philosophers, such as Wittgenstein, Goodman, and Wollheim, Shottenkirk conveyed that art is knowledge because one learns about life when looking at art. Art causes one to think differently about life, the world, and him or herself. Shottenkirk concluded that art is knowledge because similar to how research is defined, it "formulates things anew, and then passes that back into the world" (p.4).

Art can incorporate all ways of knowing, offering a culturally humble approach. It is a representation of the known, the unknown, and what is yet to be known. Therefore, art becomes a holistic way of defining reality. What is represented today can be viewed, felt, and experienced in many different forms while changing meaning and time. When addressing holism, Dreikurs (1971) noted, "So-called parts are in fact not real" (p.168). Dreikurs alluded to the idea that scientific cause and effect is not real, stating, "Purely mechanical causation, which is perhaps a mere fiction, is *equative*, but holistic causation, which is the actual process, is *creative* and accounts for the advancement that actually occurs in nature" (p.169). Art removes the concrete psychology of cognitive knowing and adds flexibility that includes the creative process of constructing reality. Art therapy has become the knowledge of self, others, and art.

Art is a representation of our experience or worldview. Art can conceptualize past and future in a present moment, making art a significant way of knowing. In the article "Research, relativism, and truth in art," Shottenkirk (2007) addressed the research culture and its relationship to art; the article reflected on the avant-garde of art and posed the question whether research in fine art parallels research in the sciences. The writer compared modernism to postmodernism and stated that the idea that knowledge is equated to scientific knowledge is nonsense. Shottenkirk suggested that artistic endeavors constitute not only a cultural practice but also add to culture, and, therefore, to personal identity and the artists' view of themselves. In other words, there is a subjective reality predicated on other ways of knowing.

In the context of Dissanayake's (1995) postmodern theory, art culture is multifaceted. Art culture did not follow the linear pattern that modernism did. Truth in modernism is universal, objective, and tolerant of diversified opinions (Shottenkirk, 2007). A postmodern art allows art therapy to approach truth through multiple ways of knowing. Gerber (2014) elaborated on the value of an art therapist, having a complete self, self-awareness of others, and a creative life, when acknowledging multiple realities as a way of being and forms of knowledge. Art therapy offers a platform where one can re-create and design one's own truth. Foucault (as cited by Martin & Barresi, 2006) elaborated that the freedom was in the re-creation of self, "by disassembling and reconstructing the habitual selves that we find ourselves to be as we are constituted in social and power relations with one another" (p.262). He expressed that care for the truth developed from the ongoing transformation of the self, as it is released and reshaped.

Although its foundation was formed under the influence of science, art therapy can address the gap in scientific knowing and generate new knowledge, as it combines scientific knowledge with symbolic ways of knowing. Through fluidity, experience, and shared social interaction, art therapy contributes to a more holistic approach. Generating new knowledge requires departing from stagnant ways of knowing toward a knowledge that can be obtained through experience. It is through the journey of self-knowledge and cultural self-identity that one obtains wisdom. The idea that "wisdom comes from self-understanding" (Martin & Barresi, 2006, p.11) is derived from the reflections of Heraclitus. Wisdom is the acknowledgment of our lived experience. Therefore, art, if approached in a holistic and culturally humble way, can offer a way to truth that may include and go beyond the scientific way of knowing, as it incorporates all one's cultural implications and ways of knowing.

## Cultural humility in assessment

Art as assessment and measurement can be used through methods of inquiry to acquire new knowledge. This can be done through social acknowledgment, art as experience, and the use of art in collaboration with multiple ways of knowing. Understanding these multifaceted ways of knowing relates to the cultural humility principle of recognizing and challenging the power imbalances for respectful partnerships and/or relationships when applied to art therapy. It is imperative for the art therapist to acknowledge biases and assumptions that arise when developing, administering, and using continuous assessments and measurements. When using art as a means of inquiry, the allure to interpret using our respective worldviews can be difficult to elude, while honoring the many ways of knowing through creative expression.

The Western epistemology of knowing has been imposed on many other cultures as the accepted form of knowledge, which dismisses and dishonors alternative ways of knowing. This ideological dominance has dismissed non-dominant ways of knowing, which could be impactful when working with and assessing culturally diverse populations. Cultural humility addresses the power imbalance through the emphasis on seeing the individual or community as rich experts and teachers on the content of culture (Tervalon & Lewis, 2018). This approach serves to honor other ways of knowing, leading the therapist to a greater cultural awareness; doing so requires moving beyond scientific interpretation in assessment and addressing other cultural factors outside of language while remaining open to the dialogue of art.

Language is often used as a measurement of assessment but often does not offer a complete description of what we know. Ray (2009) alludes to the linearity of language and describes how when specific words are repeated they become meaningless. Art as a way of knowing offers a substantial method of assessment that further describes and goes beyond language to better understand an issue. Art cannot be simply reduced to particular meanings of definitions (Ray, 2009, p.9). It has to be explored and applied as relevant to the one who creates it. It also develops a meaning for those who observe it. Because of this, a culturally humble art therapist must enter into the assessment of art with openness and acknowledgment of their emotional, social, cultural, cognitive, and theoretical approaches and connection to that particular expression. A linear and deductive approach could alter and impede the expansiveness of what is conveyed in the art. This can make using art as a form of assessment both a challenging and a useful tool. It expands allowing exploration, as opposed to deducting which can minimize and misconstrue.

Understanding the tacit meanings in art requires an art therapist practicing cultural humility to be attuned to the cultural implications within the therapeutic space. Ray (2009) reiterates the relation between tacit knowledge and expressing the inexpressible, which relates directly to art therapy. He expresses the argument of Nonaka and Takeuchi (1995), who convey that "tacit knowledge is our image of reality" and the future, in a way that is personal and difficult to communicate to others. Art therapists must be careful about underestimating the client's connection to and truth in their artistic creations, allowing the client to be centered in the assessment process by conveying their lived experience or story. When documenting an art therapy assessment, an art therapist must be careful in implying their truths to the depiction and then cataloging those implied truths and applying them to other artworks. Novice art therapists without training in cultural humility may have a tendency to state what they have viewed and interpreted as fact or Truth. It is important at the beginning of training to urge art therapist trainees to be aware of their biases, assumptions, and beliefs, while practicing writing in a subjective form, acknowledging that what is being observed is the thoughts and feelings of the observer.

Making direct meaning out of our experiences with art as an assessment loses the objectivity of expression. Those who are with an art therapist and are being assessed are offering the art therapist a view into their tacit way of knowing: "'To convert tacit knowledge into explicit knowledge means finding a way to express the inexpressible' (Nonaka, 1991, p.99), which involves finding a way to objectify the tacit dimension and thereby create explicit knowledge objects" (Ray, 2009, p.12). Art and the process of art therapy become that vehicle or "object" that reflects what is tacit knowledge, therefore becoming a form of measurement that requires delicate evaluation from a culturally humble stance.

Using multiple ways of knowing respective and inclusive of many cultures is reflective of our everyday human experience of tacit knowing. In that way, science relates to art (knowing), as it shares the same principles. Having the Western training of art observation as it relates to early art therapy theory does not supersede or illuminate the acceptance of other ways of knowing. Cultural humility elaborates on the comprehension of many ways of knowing, including scientific knowing. It also encourages an art therapist to acknowledge that the scientific way of knowing can be included, though it is not the only way to conduct assessment and measurement. Being culturally humble means recognizing that one's tacit knowledge is derived from lived experience. It is important to honor that within the context of eliciting, administering, witnessing, and interpreting assessment. Recognizing the shared commonality of the lived experience in tacit knowledge, and the explicit knowledge of formulation, could strengthen both constructs and develop a way of knowing or assessing that is holistic. In art, both the tacit and scientific ways of knowing in assessment become relevant. Cultural implications need to be considered, including tacit knowledge, and they are not at odds with scientific knowing but need to be considered to convey the whole person when assessing or developing a measurement.

Art therapy can become a strong basis for inquiry because of its holistic nature and the incorporation of other approaches. It is knowledge over time and encompasses the perception of self and others. In that way, it offers a culturally humble approach that encompasses all ways of knowing into a holistic art therapy approach that includes both art and science, tacit and explicit, while allowing for the all therapeutic aspects in the room to be a factor in client's shared story, rather than being fixed in one epistemology, which appears to have "impeded the flow of" learning (Castle, 2001, p.221).

Knowing through the experience of creative practice does not mean one must disconnect from art as an object but it includes seeing the artistic production as an action (Sutherland & Acord, 2007, p.127). This is to say that knowledge is not strictly in the work but is also in the viewer's experience of it. There is a continued need for inquiry into ways of understanding human experience from perspectives other than that of the dominant culture (Hays, 2001). Art can not only allow one to communicate and understand one's own thoughts and feelings, but it can also allow one to become aware of the thoughts and feelings of others through others' responses to the art one creates. It is in this practice that an art therapist learns the complexity of art as a way of knowing others and oneself, and understands the importance of art to social and cultural experience.

The social aspect of knowing has been dissected from scientific learning. In many cultures, knowledge is derived through social engagement, not just through individual inquiry (Hiscox & Calisch,

1998). Artistic form can reflect social experience and generate new knowledge in dynamic ways, as seen through media such as quilting, murals, music, song, and dance. Sutherland and Acord (2007) convey that art alters the way in which one experiences the world, and knowledge production emerges in the connection between the pieces of artwork and daily life. Knowing comes from the coming together that happens in the creative process. Sutherland and Acord (2007) put it simply: "Knowledge lies in encountering art, and the artwork itself exists in this knowing" (p.135).

Using this way of knowing through art requires a culturally humbly practitioner to address the cultural implications in assessment and measurement. Within art therapy, earlier pioneers and advocates for cultural inclusion in assessment conveyed many concepts that reflect a culturally humble approach. These early materials were important in laying down and continuing the discussion of cultural diversity when evaluating and exploring art made by clients/patients. One of these early materials was the Multigroup Ethnic Identity Measure (MEIM), which offered an assessment tool to assist with evaluating ethnic identity and affiliation (Roberts *et al.*, 1999).

In the therapeutic setting, both the client and the therapist's cultural background should be considered. "The beliefs, values, attitudes, feelings, and behavior of ethnic group members have a direct impact on their psychological functioning, their concept of illness, and their expression of symptoms" (Aponte, Rivers, & Whol, 1995, p.19). Art therapists and other clinicians must take this into account, along with their own biases and conceptions. This is why it is important for mental health professionals to take into account their own worldviews to better understand those of others.

Cherry (2002) used the MEIM as a pre- and post-test of a course in order to assess whether, by taking the course, students came out with a better understanding of cultural competence. Although the study was small, the results showed that the students that participated became more aware of their ethnicities. Cherry explains in her results that there is a benefit to the students who experienced a decrease during the course by stating that both positive and negative results can be evidence of self-exploration, personal growth, and becoming more aware of oneself as a cultural person. Cherry's research was valuable in relating the importance of educating art therapists and other clinical students in the role of self-understanding of culture and ethnicity to enhance cultural awareness. Cherry makes clear that this course and the research will not change one's cultural understanding and awareness for life, but can plant the seed to further investigate one's biases and understandings of one's own, as well as others', ethnic and cultural identities.

Similar to Cherry (2002), I conducted an assessment using the MEIM and the Self Identity Inventory (SII) to measure awareness of self through cultural humility in a number of graduate art therapy courses. This process highlighted the collective approach to knowing through art. It reflected a participatory action framework by asking the department, collectively, for their input on cultural humility within the program. This offered a humble stance in the implementation of a future cultural humility curriculum. Aspects of the study consisted of a pre- and post-art measure which included students being asked to complete the MEIM and the SSI, then given a pre-assignment to create a piece of art depicting their role in enhancing cultural humility in art therapy. They were then instructed to read Tervalon and Murray-Garcia, "Cultural humility versus cultural competence: A critical distinction in defining physician training outcomes in multicultural education" (1998). Prior to an in-class presentation, the participant's artwork was assessed and placed in a journal. After a presentation introducing cultural humility, its principles and its relationship to art therapy, students were asked immediately following discussion to create a post-piece of artwork depicting their current response to the question of their role in enhancing cultural humility in art therapy.

In one example of this process, upon receiving the pre- and post-art measures, the primary participant asked 11 NDNU PhD Art Therapy doctoral candidates to review each piece of artwork, hung in random order. The candidates were asked to offer a word or a short sentence reflection on their observation of each art piece created by the students in the NDNU's Art Therapy Department Master's Community and Counseling Spring 2016 class. The artwork was then placed in a collective journal and presented to the students who created the artwork for reflective analysis. Through collaborative discussion of the completed journal and the written reflections from the PhD candidates, it was derived that most pre-assessment art depicted a contained, reserved, individualized and growing understanding of cultural humility. The post-assessment art appeared more expansive, collective, whole, and intensified (see Figures 2.2, 2.3, and 2.4).

*Figure 2.2 Pre- and post-assessment artwork Student 1*

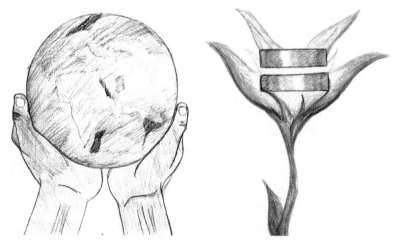

*Figure 2.3 Pre- and post-assessment artwork Student 2*

*Figure 2.4 Pre- and post-assessment artwork Student 3*

Upon completion of their journal entry, each participant was given the opportunity to offer an interview responding to the post-assessment questions or to respond via email. The post-assessment questionnaire asked participants (1) Is there a need to enhance cultural humility in the art therapy department? (2) What degree of influence do you believe cultural humility currently has on the profession of art therapy? Four students offered their responses via email prior to viewing the collective journal. Six students offered their response to the above questions in class while reviewing the collective journal. Ten students offered their written reflection on (3) Describe your experience with the art: pre-prompt, post-prompt, and completed journal. One student agreed to have her responses voice recorded as English was her second language and she had difficulty writing what she wanted to express.

Responses ranged through "I loved seeing the completed book and how the second drawings seemed to grow in depth, intensity, and passion. There was a sense of unity in the second drawings and an excitement for integrating cultural humility rather than the general reaction from the 1st drawing" (Student 1, 2016); "I think it [cultural humility] influences every aspect of art therapy—how we practice; how we see our clients, our relationships with ourselves and our communities. Though it influences art therapy, we need to remind ourselves of it more" (Student 2, 2016); "Even more powerful was the completed journal viewing experience. Seeing everyone's collective work, the shift felt very real. The visuals exuded so much feeling as a collective body of work" (Student 3, 2016); "Yes, there is absolutely a need to enhance cultural humility in art therapy. In order to work with clients, we study all the techniques, theories, specific populations, disorders, etc. However, all of what we learn has to be able to be applied to/catered to whomever we encounter. We need to be open to all cultures, understanding power/privilege, etc." (Student 4, 2016).

The data collected in the pre- and post-art assessments and the post-questionnaire art journal reflections were used to evaluate the necessity and strategies in implementing a cultural humility curriculum into the Art Therapy Master's program. The data were also used to present findings to faculty and created a future training tool. Recommendations were given to the department chair for future implementation. A more immediate and practical recommendations application included continued presentations and introductions of cultural humility, with the concept incorporated in courses offered in the program.

## The application of cultural humility in art therapy research

Developing new paradigms in thinking, such as incorporating the principles of cultural humility, an art therapist can include and move from scientific knowing to experiential knowing, shifting outside the cause-and-effect paradigm. The experiential knowing process bolsters cultural humility and encourages identity development in art therapists, both as professionals and as individuals (Jackson, 2016).

When adopting a culturally humble approach to research it can be used as a collective and transformative learning experience. By fostering both collective and individualistic perspectives simultaneously the research can become balanced in depicting both self-reflective and mutual relationships of others within the research, including the primary researcher, the individual participants, and the group as collaborators. Within this approach, the interrelatedness becomes illuminated through the art in the research. This increases the acceptance of both Western and non-Western ways of knowing that can present themselves in addressing many different perspectives. In this method, each contributor is allowed and encouraged to exert their tacit knowledge through the art, then is able to recreate their truth in the art as a form of wisdom. An art therapist open to this approach offers curiosity, creativity, and an integrated experience.

## The engagement of project and participants

Before contemplating engagement in a project, an art therapist should self-reflect on the purpose of the project. There may be a particular interest held by the principal investigator that is not held by those they are engaging in the research with. The same can be said the other way around. What is important is to do some reflective work to explore intentions and whether they are mutually beneficial or will be a detriment to the participants/collaborators. The needs of the participants/collaborators should be considered and the art therapist is encouraged to openly convey to the participants/collaborators the ways they can offer their assistance. The cultural implications between all parties should be evaluated. For example: Will the participants/collaborators be acknowledged in the research and how will they be enhanced or made relevant? Is there a bias that is already being conveyed at the onset of the research? What safeguards are being put in place for implicit biases that may arise?

If working with a group of primary researchers, the self-reflective process can be even more relevant as each individual may be coming into the research with a different intention and world lens. An exercise that can be helpful in guiding this process is as follows:

- Sit within your research group.

- First, reflect on why you are engaging in this project.

- Second, come together and share dialogue about commonality and purpose.

- Next, create artwork reflecting your shared process.

- Finally, examine the art and discuss next steps in honoring the process and engagement of your research project:

    - In what ways are each of you wise?

    - What wisdom can be found in your participants/collaborators...participants'/collaborators' art?

    - How will you take this knowledge into your research project? What is the need?

After examining the purpose of the research, a culturally humble art therapist engages the participants as experts or collaborators in the research process. Both parties have knowledge based on their lived experience that becomes relevant in the research process. There is also an opportunity to offer training or tasks to collaborators/participants that empower them to have a partnership in the study.

It can be easy to collect art and perceive it as data. Honoring the art as an experience of the creator allows the art to not only be seen as scientific data that will be quantifiably analyzed, but also as tacit knowledge offered by those in collaboration. That offering then becomes a way of viewing the art as a qualifying aspect of data analyses.

## An example of cultural humility in research

In 2015–2016, I conducted a collective research study titled "Acquiring new knowledge through art self-exploration and collective journaling to enhance cultural humility in art therapy" (Jackson, 2016). This study explored ways of knowing through the presence and/or absence of the wisdom depicted by Black women in art therapy and related fields of study. Thirteen Black female art therapists and seven Black female professionals in related fields of practice were asked to contribute to collective journals with the one prompt of offering their depiction of their experience of "being a Black woman in your field of study as it relates to cultural humility." The research focused on an inquiry into how the wisdom of Black women currently serves as part of the philosophy, theory, and practice of art therapy. Through this project, many revelations relevant to this inquiry were acknowledged, with the focus on cultural humility, which became the focal point of this research.

One question specified in the introduction of this research was, "Can looking at the lived experience of Black female art therapists and Black women in related fields of study illuminate tacit and interrelational ways of knowing in art therapy?" The participatory action component that was part of the inquiry process of this research allowed the research question to evolve as the collaborators offered their contributions. The results of this research speak to this question, as the women depicted their lived experiences in ways that validated the collective while acknowledging each woman's individual tacit way of knowing through art and word. The collaborators, each identifying as Black or African American, gave a perspective that is useful in a field dominated by one specific ethnic and gender group. In this research, many areas of knowing were addressed. To ensure the validity of this research, I did not offer a definitive conclusion nor recount my own biases. The discussion of this research was designed to offer an alternative perspective to ways of knowing particularly in the field of art therapy. To foster cultural humility, the research depicts a small sample of interrelated individuals connected through culture; they share intimate and strong emotions to their lived experience. Although some of the experiences are shared, they do not speak for all as similar experiences, professions, and attributes. Offering a pre- and post-test (MEIM and SSI), cycling back to the collaborators to ask their evaluation of the journals, sharing findings, and having ongoing interviews with the women of this study offered validity checks (Kapitan, 2010).

Through this journaling process, I, along with the collaborators, appeared to engage in transformative learning by being able to collectively communicate while participating in a creative process and self-reflection. Through data analysis, specific areas related to the initial research hypothesis were extracted. Concepts such as balance, circular process, self-reflection, collective, social awareness, truth, recognizing biases, narrative knowing, and the relevance of Western ideology were reflected within the content of the collective journals, written reflections, self-journals, and interviews. Together these areas of data collection encompass a oneness that summarized the collective process of this research project. Cultural humility encompasses being vigilant of individual goals, awareness, worldview, and collective influences (values, beliefs, and assumptions) with humility. Wholeness includes both one's individual and collective selves. Becoming culturally humble, with humility, love, and courage, within one's whole self, occurs in continuous, sustained self-reflection (art, journal, intrapersonal dialogue) and persistent cultural proficiency (skill, knowledge, practice). This is all done in balance (interrelatedness). It includes allowing those with whom one collaborates to be seen and heard while acknowledging their whole presence. Being culturally humble must be a transformative learning process: "learning to integrate intellectual understanding (knowledge) with emotional understanding (affect)" (Jun, 2010, p.9). As art therapists engaging in both individual and collective worldviews through art, while also engaging in continued cultural diversity training, individuals can participate in the knowledge and effect of transformative learning.

## Commitment to engage in a lifelong process

The point of interest of this research was cultural humility, heuristic research, self-reflection, and reflections of a group. Culture has been defined in numerous ways. Although Paz (1991) used the term civilization to reflect what was defined as a community, Tervalon (2015) contextualized the statement to refer to culture and identity. In this study, Tervalon's definition was used to define culture. This definition is inclusive of many areas depicted by Paz. Although the culture of this group is similar, the reflections of the group varied according to each woman's experience. The images communicated and reverberated off one another, sometimes in harmony and sometimes in discord. Universally, all of the women in this study displayed the quality of being humble. Cultural humility is "marked by modesty in behavior, attitude or spirit; showing patience, gentleness, and moderation about one's own abilities and values" (M. Tervalon, personal communication, March 3, 2012). Some women spoke with conviction, others with tenacity and strength. These are communication styles that are often perceived as anger or aggression when associated with Black women (Watch Cut Video, 2016). When reflecting on these images from an open stance, one can feel the compassion and empathy that shows up in all the images and words. There is a feeling of needing to be listened to and understood.

The development of the journal used in this study allowed many of the participants to construct their truth and make themselves visible. In cultural humility, the ongoing transformation of self allows for truth to develop. As supported by Jun (2010), "In order for an affective transformative process to occur, individuals need to accept themselves as they are. It is necessary that they do not judge or censor themselves to be aware of inner experience" (p.263). The process of creating a visual depiction of their lived experience as Black women, as it relates to cultural humility, offered "methods to facilitate affective transformation such as narrative writing, imagery, and silence" (Jun, 2010, p.264). Jun illuminated the effectiveness of art in transformative learning as she shared how knowledge cannot be gained through words alone, but that imagery, memory, and reflection can facilitate transformative learning about compassion (p.264). Doing exercises using these aspects similar to the collective journal and the self-journal can assist in stopping "automatic inappropriate thinking"; it can "allow individuals to consider other people's pain equal to their own" (p.266). Jun described the affective transformation process, which "begins when a practitioner takes the personal affective position in an attempt to feel the client's feelings through remembering their own painful experience" (p.266). This relates to the description of humility. Jun described deconstructing inappropriate thinking patterns, such as hierarchical, dichotomous, and linear patterns, by continued practice, which supports the lifelong engagement of cultural humility in relation to reflective art therapy.

It was clear from the written reflection and artistic depictions of the collaborators in this research that they shared common revelations based on their shared ethnicity, but also spoke to the openness and equality of all individuals. Jun (2010) reported that "as long as individuals with multicultural backgrounds only want to be inclusive of what they value and believe and exclude other identities they do not value, achieving equity and justice for all people will not be feasible" (p.263). Through the reflections of the collaborators and my own self-reflective work, it became apparent that the shared reflections were not to show a preference for the group but to express emotions related to personal and social distress not typically illuminated. Jun also stated, "In-group favoritism may occur without intergroup comparison or outgroup negativity" (p.281). Although this research focused on one group, it did not mean to alienate others. Jun stated that social change starts with one person and that groups with appropriate thinking styles can affect others: "Groups of individuals become a society by taking a small step each day to deconstruct inappropriate hierarchical and dichotomous thinking" (p.281). This group of individuals is small in comparison to the field of art therapy, but the aspiration is that its sentiments and images cause others to self-reflect and alter inappropriate thinking patterns.

## Implications of cultural humility-focused research

This research can offer an elaborate, integrated holistic approach to the field. Curiosity sparks creativity; being inquisitive about one's self and others is one of the components of cultural humility (Tervalon, 2015). Having the comprehension that one does not know all leaves room for growth and opens the door for creative expansion. Art as an integrated experience allows art therapists to be with their clients as they embark on their creative journey. If the art therapist is there to experience the journey, instead of simply to dictate its direction, it may allow the client to be empowered enough to interrupt their own story. Acknowledging that there are other ways of knowing outside of the dominant culture may expand the practice and education of art therapy so that it is inclusive of collective approaches, as well as other ethnic groups' experiences. This inclusive approach can encourage and serve as a gateway to bring art therapy to a broader client base, as well as acquire educators and practitioners from other cultural and ethnic backgrounds. Collective learning was strongly demonstrated through this research. Learning from one another can be as imperative for art therapists as learning from the ones we serve. Collective learning reinforces the human connectedness of cultural humility in art therapy; the artwork in this study identified ways we are alike as well as our common goals as art therapists, regardless of cultural background. It also highlights our diversity, which is equally important and once again expresses balance.

The study's findings encourage practitioners to be aware of who they are, where they are, and who shows up in the room. With discussions of cultural humility in art therapy, art therapists may view clients in a broader context by viewing their needs through a cultural lens. Using a collective journal also offers an example of collective materials to consider in the practice of art therapy. I believe in acknowledging other ways of knowing as well as "respect, discipline, and humility" (Rubin, 2001).

## Recommendations for future research projects

Supporting Boston (2014, p.68), the majority of my work and motivation as an art therapist has been to contribute to and improve cultural humility in the therapeutic practice. My Master's research focused on culture, art, and self-identity. I continued to take up with these topics in this study, striving to examine and enhance cultural humility by looking at other ways of knowing through a collective and self-reflection. I am hopeful that this topic will continue to spark interest in others. This work can offer a foundational approach that should be further explored. Both micro and macro levels of society were depicted in this research, along with the impact they have on the individual and the group. Collectivist and individualist perspectives were offered, which validated the need to acknowledge both as ways of knowing. Also illuminated in this study were foundational social issues and the effects of these issues on art therapy treatment. These aspects may assist researchers to examine diverse communities' access to art therapy. The women's guidance may offer a culturally humble approach to clients, which may present an alternative to practitioners' current approaches and which again could be pursued in future research. I recognize my gift of being an art therapist and my ability to teach others how to hone and develop their skills. Art therapy is growing; it is a wonderful time to be a part of this movement and to be part of a growing group of professionals advancing the field through research while contributing to standards across the country.

The other chapters in this book will highlight the key components of cultural humility in art therapy as discovered in the above-mentioned research, beginning with the metaphor of the body as a way of examining assessment, research, and scholarly work that offers a platform of discovery in cultural humility, following with the metaphor of the eyes: our world lens that guides our art therapy practice, policy, and theory. Next the metaphor of our hands, the way in which we reach out to communities and offer our services to develop mutual relationships. Then the metaphor of our heart, which holds our compassion to advocate for all in the service of diversity, equity, and inclusion with others and the field of art therapy. And then the metaphor of the circle: the circular movement of cultural humility which is depicted by mandalas that describe the revisiting of introspection. Finally, we cover symbolic representation in developing metaphor in art therapy pedagogy and making meaning to foster cultural humility in advocacy within institutional accountability.

## REFLECTIVE PERSPECTIVE

(Transcription of research collaborator's video response to post-survey of my dissertation research project)

*Collective Study Collaborator (CSC)*: I anticipated getting the journal for a while, so I was waiting for it to come. Checking by the mail, I was excited about the opportunity. It was also a mystery, so that was cool to have it be unknown what I was going to be receiving. Also it was hard not to plan what I was going to reflect on cuz I wasn't sure what I needed to reflect on. I knew it had something to do with humility and culture but I wasn't sure what the question was exactly. So it was nice being a mystery and relying on what would happen intuitively when I got the journal.

*Primary Collaborator (PC)*: So what were your thoughts after receiving the journal?

CSC: After I received it and read the instructions and I got the opportunity...I didn't realize I would get the opportunity to read everybody else's portion. I was impressed. I had an emotional experience too because I realized I am not alone. That my feelings and my experience as an African American therapist resonated with a lot of people. And although our participant group was I think under 20 of us, but I was thinking this is what we get to share and say to each other that I don't get to talk about. Everything resonated with me that was said one way or another. And this was something we need to talk to people about. So, it was nice.

PC: So how would you explain your experience with the journal?

CSC: It was intense because I had to read it and go through. I had to put it down; I had to come back to it. I had to do a draft of what was happening for me because it was good to have it be in the form of art because the words were not coming because it was such an emotional experience and I'm pretty good with words. And I thought this is hard. This is hard because it was so deep. Then I had asked myself how vulnerable do I want to be. Seeing how vulnerable everyone else was encouraged me.

PC: Is there wisdom or way of knowing that is part of being an African American woman?

CSC: Yeah I think there is and um a theme that I saw...I am one of the ones that was that was close to the last to get the journal so I got to see everyone else's, and what I saw was this idea of birthing something forward that is within us. And the whole birthing process, the mothering process, and the caring process, the producing and the caring for what you produce. And then what you're producing as a Black woman is judged by the world in a different way. And what I saw was this breaking out of not being judged anymore. Let us be our judge. Let us manifest the way we need to. That was beautiful.

PC: What is the relationship to art (with what you just said)?

CSC: I think the relationship is that words cannot encapsulate everything that we have to express, it can't. I almost felt that as I was reading everyone's entry and then I worked on my own. I mean I sat back after looking at my own self and was in awe about what I put. Because that was not planned. It's just something in me that came out versus you writing a paper. So it's that intra-psychic work that only art can bring about.

*PC*: Are there any sentiments that you would like to share with future viewers of the journal?

*CSC*: Just to...and this is for those who are able to look at what we've done, just the collaborative Spirit of it all was beautiful. And that all of our voices to me creates one voice and that's what I walked away with from my portion. This is the voice of a few but it's also the voice of many.

*PC*: If anything, what would you improve about the journal process?

*CSC*: I would of liked to have had it longer and had more pages.

*PC*: Would you engage in similar research in the future?

*CSC*: Definitely.

*PC*: Would you be willing to participate in a future workshop or seminar to discuss your participation in this research.

*CSC*: Yes, definitely.

*PC*: Is there anything else you would like to share about your thoughts or feelings about African American women's wisdom and its place in the field of art therapy?

*CSC*: I think it's something that needs to be tapped into on a deeper level. I think that...of course I brought it back to into the educational realm. And I was thinking, why is it that we don't have a theory of practice? I get multicultural is used, but obviously, from what I saw of what we did as collaborators, there could be a whole 'nother theory. A whole 'nother way of knowing. A whole new therapy that is created. In order for that to happen we have to come together. And I know we have to quantify it. Try to quantify what is within us. And I think that research and this kind of research is the way to go.

*PC*: Thank you.

*CSC*: Thank you!

## RESPONSE ART

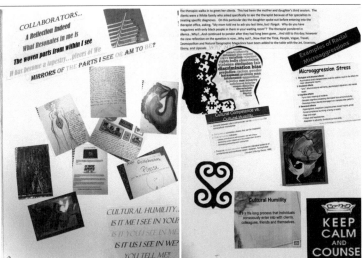

*Figure 2.5a and 2.5b, Collective Study Collaborator Art 017*

# REFLECTIVE EXERCISE B: **TRAVELING JOURNAL**

◼ **Goal:** Art identity exploration.

◼ **Materials:** A journal, structured art materials that can be facilitated in chosen journal.

◼ **Prompt:** Shared journal activity:

1. Pose a question related to your identity aspects. For example: What brings me into my field of work? What can I offer to those I serve? What parts of my identity impact my practice and how?

2. Once you have posed a question to explore, create a piece of artwork related to your inquiry.

3. When you are done, journal about your experience.

4. Try sharing your journal with an intimate group of others, asking them to engage in the same process.

5. When everyone you have asked has collaborated, invite the group to come together to view the journal in its entirety and dialogue about the journey through this method. Pay attention to judgments that may arise. Follow the art as a way of knowing self and other. Look for commonalities, deviations, and overlap. Try to remain open as others share their lived experience, expressing both challenges and moments of encouragement/inspiration.

# CHAPTER 3

# Cultural Humility in Art Therapy Practice

*Eyes: Worldview, How We Perceive the World and Practice in It*

Recovery + Cultural Humility #016

Cultural humility vs. cultural competent made more sense to me. My recovery program encourages DAILY self-reflection and a willingness to CHECK myself for intolerance, impatience, selfishness, self-centeredness, etc. .. It's very much like "...a lifelong commitment to self-evaluation and self-critique..."

My journey continues...

Cultural Humility keeps me mindful of my recovery program in the day-to-day grind of advocating, educating, and be learning more about the Consumers I am responsible for serving and their challenges of power imbalances.

Cultural Humility / 12-Steps keep me mindful that the Consumers are the teachers. I must be honest, acknowledge, and be OK with telling the Consumers I serve, "I don't know / understand because I am not the expert, you are."

The 12-Steps have taught me to honor and respect each person's beliefs; to live life on life terms without judgement or fear. The principles of Cultural Humility keeps me mindful of my recovery program.

Cultural Humility is yet another step towards my spiritual journey /growth and JOY!

*All things are lessons God would have me learn. (ACIM, Lesson 193)*

*Figure 3.1 My Story: Recovery + Cultural Humility, Collective Study Collaborator Art 016*

## Developing our lens

The eyes can be representative of our way of seeing the world; they are essentially our lens, the way in which we view the world, or our worldview. Calisch (2003, p.13) supports this notion, recommending the moving of art therapy from a more Eurocentric worldview: "Despite our present immersion in Eurocentric thinking and practice, our profession is beginning to transform educational curricula and to become a profession with a more ethno-relativistic style of thinking in order to provide the highest quality of care to our clients."

Over the past ten years, the field of art therapy has made strides toward this effort. As the training of future art therapists can assist in continuing to shift this worldview dynamic from Eurocentric to ethnocentric, this is echoed extensively by Kapitan (2015). Chapter 7 of this book will provide a closer examination, offering a curriculum which is culturally humble, diverse, and inclusive. In this chapter, the focus of practice in art therapy using a culturally humble lens will be explored. This exploration will assist in balancing the discussion of being an effective multicultural counselor, which is often interpreted as someone who has a specialty in working with others outside the dominant culture. The assumption that once a counselor has mastered all the characteristics pertaining to a variety of cultural, racial, and ethnic groups, it will then allow them to possess the skill to be an effective multicultural counselor can result in a multicultural "cookbook" provider (Speight et al., 1991). Multicultural counseling should not be looked upon as an "extra skill" but an integrated component of all forms of therapy. Sadeghi, Fischer, and House (2003) add to this by stating:

> The textbook and research findings and psychological theories often contained culture-specific assumptions. Some of these assumptions include a universal definition of what constitutes "normal" behavior, individualism as preferable to collectivism, independence as more desirable than dependence, an emphasis on understanding linear thinking where each cause has an effect and each effect a cause, and the paradigm wherein counselors change an individual to fit the system rather than changing the system to the individual. (p.180)

This describes a culturally humble counselor, one who understands that all individuals providers work with have cultural identities, lived experiences, and tacit knowledge that may or may not align with their own. This is the underlying concept of the cultural humility principles, that one must work to readdress the power imbalance in the patient–provider dynamic, in addition to developing mutually beneficial partnerships with communities on behalf of individuals and defined populations (Tervalon & Murray-Garcia, 1998).

As culture assumptions are found in art therapy, Hocoy (2002) states that art therapy has also been derived from Western therapeutic traditions and it is important for the field to acknowledge that in order to make progressions in cross-culturalism. He also states that art therapists can do a few things to maximize the likelihood of the ethical and effective treatment of individuals from a non-Euro-American culture, such as engaging in rigorous and honest self-examination as to their cultural competency, continual professional development in multicultural competency through readings, workshops, and consulting with members of the community in which the therapist is working (Hocoy, 2002). Again, going back to cultural humility principles, a culturally humble art therapist engages in a lifelong process of critical self-reflection and self-critique. Hocoy (2002) notes that art therapy can become even more valuable in cross-cultural therapy if it moves beyond its Western roots.

Perhaps the most central issue concerns the potential for art therapy to perpetuate Western cultural imperialism. Hamrick and Byma (2017) address how dominant whiteness in art therapy negatively affects white art therapists by limiting their social skills, self-awareness, and ability to engage in productive dialogue about race and other structures of oppression with clients and peers (p.107). The history of Western therapeutic traditions is replete with instances in which legitimate cultural expressions are pathologized, marginalized, or misinterpreted. Art therapy in its conscious consideration of these issues has the unique opportunity to depart from this heritage and to serve as a tool of cultural enrichment rather than oppression (Hocoy, 2002)

In the article "Multicultural training in art therapy: past, present, and future," Calisch (2003) attempts to bring together art therapy and multicultural training. She relays that there are several additional issues that remain matters of concern in both educational and clinical art therapy settings. These matters of concern are (1) lack of clearly defined standards or content for multicultural education and cultural competence; (2) failure to encourage students to contextualize persons in their cultural settings; (3) lack of or haphazard application of research information relevant to multicultural therapeutic practice; (4) professional practice that is characterized by an increasing separation between research and practice, lack of multicultural training of educators, and lack of diversity in regard to both gender and culture within the profession. Many of the concerns can be seen as relevant today, as the field of art therapy continues to seek ways of integrating inclusion, diversity, and equity across education, practice, and research. Suggesting that creative cultural competence begins with learning about other cultures supports the skills, which are adopted in cultural competence training (Calisch, 2003). Aligning with cultural humility, Calisch acknowledges that this is a lifelong task and that learning about oneself in context with other persons who may differ in some degree is part of this task. Although it is instructive for art therapists to enlighten themselves by participating in a variety of therapeutic relationships, it may not be to the benefit of the client. It is also important for the therapist to have a significant amount of training and experience required to provide culturally competent information. The amount of training in multiculturalism is equally important, as is the willingness for self-knowledge and self-exploration around one's own cultural identity and how one relates to others (Calisch, 2003). It is encouraged in cultural humility to be curious and inquire from a client. If done in a way that does not imply acquiring facts to fill out an assessment form, it can display interest to the client and imply to the client that you are willing to learn more about them without making assumptions. This requires allowing the client to share what they are comfortable with, without harshly probing and coming across as accusatory. When discussing treatment efficacy, Calisch (2003) asserted that the most effective treatment approaches for minority clients should include valuing diversity; multicultural competence; facilitation of internalization of an accurate, positive, and affirming racial identity; and validation of experiences and promotion of empowerment, self-empathy, and mutuality. To address the power imbalance and racial biases that often and historically occur with underrepresented populations this should be especially considered, while understanding that all therapeutic exchange requires the same effective treatment, as all populations can be judged, assumed, and biased.

Through years of revision the AATA *Ethical Principles for Art Therapists* states, (7.0) Multicultural and Diversity Competence in art therapy refers to the capacity of art therapists to continually acquire cultural, diversity awareness and knowledge with regard to self and others, and to successfully apply these skills in practice with clients. Art therapists maintain multicultural and diversity competence to provide treatment interventions and strategies that include awareness of and responsiveness to cultural issues. AATA *Ethical Principles for Art Therapists* (2013) (7.1–7) state:

> ...do not discriminate...ensure sensitivity...and learn about the beliefs of people in any given cultural group in order to provide culturally relevant interventions and treatment... aware of their own values and beliefs...education about and seek to understand the nature of social diversity and oppression (with respect across all cultural identities)...acquire knowledge and information about the specific cultural group(s) with which they are working and the strengths inherent in those cultural groups (with varying responses to group norms)... art therapists engage in culturally sensitive supervision or education, seek assistance from members of that culture, and make referrals to professionals who are knowledgeable about the cultures when it is in the best interest of the clients to do so.

Although it is apparent that understanding the affects of different ethnicities and cultures is important to the therapeutic practice, many still separate multiculturalism as the practice of a therapist from the dominant group that shares its own ethnic background, culture, and values, engaging with an "other." And those that fall outside of the dominant group are viewed as persons the therapist must relate to on a multicultural level. Should we have one set of theories and skills for this dominant group and another for everyone else who does not fall in this category?

All counseling is cross-cultural or multicultural because all humans differ in terms of cultural background, values, lifestyle, and lived experiences. The ability to work with another individual—who by definition is a separate and distinct entity—is a basic counseling skill, not reserved only for those who choose to specialize in multicultural counseling. All art therapists can become effective if offering a culturally humble approach, which honors the client as a rich expert of their own lived experience, providing patient-centered care. And, while practicing becoming culturally humble clinicians, art therapists cannot dismiss the social contexts we live in. Although this social context may vary by region and country, aspects of identity, particularly race or ethnic identity, become important in the context of therapeutic practice, relationships, and image. In therapy, issues of identity are a dominant theme. Because we (art therapists) work with images in art therapy, self-expression, unconscious and conscious communication, identity, and the naming of identity are powerfully charged subjects (Campbell *et al.*, 1999). In the chapter "Living Color in Art Therapy" (Campbell *et al.*, 1999), authors Vickey Barber and Jean Campbell address color and identity as two interlocked parts of self, one psychological and one social, quoting Mama (1995, p.1):

> I use the concept of subjectivity instead of the psychological term identity and "self" to indicate my rejection of the dualistic notion of psychological and social spheres as essential separate territories; one internal and the other external to the person. Instead, I regard both as being continuously constituted and changing, as being locked in a recessive relationship of mutual advancing production and change.

Within Western culture, ethnic identity is interrelated in an individual's whole being. Separating the two often denies the other. Below, the term intersectionality will be explored as a way to comprehend the deep interlocking of this aspect of identity as well as other aspects. The significance is allowing the individual to be the expert and have the opportunity to identify themselves.

An essential aspect of a culturally humble clinician is understanding the importance of allowing the client to bring their whole self into the therapeutic space; in whatever form that may present itself at any given time. Being comfortable with not always leading from the front and collaborating with the client can allow the client to tell their story without the clinician's interruptions. Often, therapists, particularly those from more directive theoretical orientations, come into a session with an agenda and steer the engagement in the direction they feel is best based on their own judgment, without consulting with the client regarding their needs. This behavior can cause a therapist to interrupt, redirect, and sabotage what could have been an impactful space for acceptance, empathy, and guidance. It is imperative to allow for the client and the image to be a part of their own healing process to offer empowerment and shift the power imbalance:

> The art therapy process allows images of the self to be created and recreated in as many ways as is necessary for the person to tell [their] story of who [they are] and how [they] come to be how [they are]. This includes [their] fantasy self as well as aspects of [themselves] in different times, spaces and in relation to others. (Campbell *et al.*, 1999, p.27)

All aspects of a client cannot be seen solely as separate entities but also as parts of the whole, moving the discussion of intersectionality as a relevant aspect of culturally awareness and humility.

Intersectionality continues to be a significant cornerstone when addressing cultural awareness. Many have offered a comprehensive examination into the ethical application, framework, and discussion of intersectionality in art therapy (Junge, 2014; Kuri, 2017; Talwar, 2010). After conceptualizing the development of intersectionality derived from feminist women of color and lesbian scholars, Talwar (2010) investigates the implications of intersectionality for art therapy, urging therapists to think critically about the multidimensional aspects of identity and the political and social systems that impact those identities, expressing the need to examine the role of oppression, the impact of popular culture, and visual media influences. Her words reverberate a cultural humble stance as she expresses attention to the power imbalance in the therapeutic practice and the field of art therapy, further stating, "knowledge and power are linked" (Talwar, 2010, p.13). The critical self-reflective process of art therapy can elicit an understanding of the foundation in which a therapist positions themselves in relation to the interconnectedness of identity, social positioning, theoretical framework, knowledge base, and the many ramifications which form our presentation of self. An art therapist bringing this into awareness can shift the power dynamic within practice, training, assessment, and research.

Recounting the impact of "internalized sexism" in art therapy, Junge (2014) begins by applying what was derived to address "societies oppression of women...to everybody" (p.25). She recounts art therapy beginnings as a "women's profession" and the "establishment of organized art therapy by white women" who were told they needed to adhere to society's gender roles of that time (p.26). She concludes by stating that "to recognize the cultural oppression that gives rise to internalized sexism as it intersects with art therapy's identity is to be more fully cognizant of the difficulties art therapy and art therapist have had to encounter to survive" (p.27). Although this may be relevant, when examining the impact on the individuals who practice and receive art therapy services, a clinician should keep in mind the toll on those whose intersections of identity are oppressed in predominantly all derivatives of their lived experience and how organized art therapy has impacted and facilitated that oppression. In expressing how important it is "to understand how intersecting social locations (race, class, gender, sexuality, disability, or religion) determine one's place in society, and how some benefit from unearned privileges at the cost of others" Kuri (2017, p.118) relates the need "to have an understanding of whiteness for white people to avoid co-opting intersectionality to support their social or professional position, potentially perpetuating oppressive practices." Again, referring to Talwar (2015) and echoing cultural humility, Kuri (2017) concludes, "Above all...[the art therapist] must make a commitment to ongoing reflexivity, which means working toward a critical awareness of their social location and assumptions with respect to power, privilege, and oppression" (p.120). Applying the principles of cultural humility requires an ongoing critical self-reflective process to examine one's biases, assumptions, and beliefs. This moves the invested and authentic art therapist toward an awareness that is culturally relevant, derived in integrity, social justice-focused, and fosters a multidimensional worldview lens.

## Cultural variables in policy, practice, and theory

What is a variable? In *Merriam-Webster's Online Dictionary* (2019e), a variable is defined as "able or likely to change or be changed: not always the same" (def. 1). Multiple cultural variables exist and need to be considered in the art therapy process; one could write a book with a chapter dedicated to each variable. Some of those variables are age, gender, sex, political affiliation, religion, ethnicity, social economic background, language, family structure/parenting, climate, war/peacetime, natural disaster area, location (country), images/symbols, traditions/rituals, body movement or restriction, facial expression, tone of voice, process of art-making, beliefs, behavior, words/terms, materials, language, and self-identity of the client and therapist. This section will focus on a few of these variables and their influence on art therapy practice.

Why should we consider cultural variables when using art in the therapeutic process? As art therapists it is our responsibility to acknowledge that cultural influences are a part of human development as stated by Trommsdorff (2002, p.3): "human development takes place in a given cultural context; it is both affected by culture and affects culture." Integrated with cultural humility, understanding how culture affects our viewpoints, process, and our clients will make for a more healthy and balanced approach to using art in therapy.

In early approaches to culture in therapy, many therapists from dominant groups wrote about their personal observations and projections of other cultures to understand others' cultural norms. Most of what we see in art therapy history, when we look at how culture was addressed, comes from a white male dominant perspective, as examined in Talwar (2010, p.11): "In the field of art therapy the dominant perspective on human relationships is largely derived from male, Eurocentric teaching." McNiff (2009) refers to this. "In cross-cultural research, a fundamental taboo is the projection of a personal theory of behavior and values onto other cultural groups" (p.101). McNiff reflects on how Darwin and early psychotherapy views insisted that all humans shared the same universal principles, "His concepts of evolution influenced Freud who saw both the individual and the human race as developing according to universal principles" (p.102), ignoring the cultural variables that we now know affect individuals and humans as a whole and the importance of intersectionality. Although there are universal aspects of art, when creating art and using it as a therapeutic tool for communications, there are also particulars that are conveyed according to the different cultural variables, as addressed by McNiff (2009):

> Of all expressive modes, language most clearly presents cultural differences, whereas the visual arts, music, and dance are more interchangeable and universal...there has been an interdependence between universal and particular forms of communications. Creativity is the drive towards the particular... (p.102)

A few of these cultural variables are mentioned by McNiff, including "body movement, facial expression, and tone of voice...war versus peacetime; poverty versus affluence; climate; and regional ritual traditions," as he shares how "these culturally specific experiences manifest themselves in both art and group process" (p.105). Cultural variables prompt an art therapist to search for resources to assist with learning about these cultural ramifications, along with sharply examining their own body language and movement within the therapeutic space, which may be a reaction to others' cultural variables.

Another cultural variable is the self-identity of the art therapist. Many of the writers of the *Art Therapy Journal* series *Stories of Art Therapists of Color* reflected on their process of identifying themselves and the effect the process had on their therapeutic practice (Boston, 2005; Boston & Short, 2006; Doby-Copeland, 2006b; Farris, 2006; Hocoy, 2006; Joseph, 2006, Levy, 2006; Lumpkin, 2006; Potash, 2005). Doby-Copeland (2006b) wrote about how identifying awareness in tangent with her own cultural experience, helped herself and other professionals work more effectively with their clients. "Again, my cultural knowledge gave me better information on the patient that wasn't stereotypical or biased. I like to think that my consciousness through the art and my awareness of culture helped my patients be more clearly 'seen'" (p.82).

In the same series, Lumpkin (2006) shared her experience with self-identity as it related to the different aspects of her life and the populations she worked with. She stated, "This cultural exploration of my identity as an art therapist revealed a few things...as I acknowledge, respect and seemingly accept my cultural heritage and placement in art therapy...more often in my professional placement... either sacrificing parts of myself or questioning my identity and belongings" (p.37). She concludes, "Lastly, I realize that being an art therapist is not one-dimensional; nor does one size fits all. In other words, there is no single definition that captures all that an art therapist is; nor does each art therapist define him or herself the same" (p.38). Being able to reflect on one's own culture while recognizing that we are all different, including those we work with, culturally humble art therapists can enter the therapeutic relationship with respect, empathy, and a healthy inquisitiveness to learn about each other.

More recently, cultural variables of gender and sexual orientation have been included in the larger conversations of culturally specific treatment. This has been absent in literature and cultural training for a while in art therapy, as much early training focused on ethnic identity. Pelton-Sweet and Sherry (2008) state that it is important to note that "many factors that may affect the coming out process, such as age, ethnicity, and gender" (p.171), again emphasizing how many similar variables affect many different cultural contexts. As in all cultural concepts, Pelton-Sweet and Sherry (2008, p.172) emphasize "understanding, homophobia, and heterosexism, understanding sexual identity development, being non-judgmental and respecting differences, and being willing to discuss any aspect of their clients' lives." Jackson *et al.* expand upon this aspect of cultural identity: "art therapists should be aware of existing assumptions regarding this community; failure to do so can hinder growth and possibly cause harm" (2018, p.111), adding the importance of becoming aware of the heterosexual assumption that can negate an essential cultural variable such as the ongoing "coming out" process of our clients (Jackson *et al.*, 2018).

Hiscox and Calisch (1998) address other cultural variables. In Nadia Ferrara's chapter in this book about her experience doing "Art therapy with a Cree Indian boy," she supported the concept that cultural perception, as part of self-identity, is a concern and is relevant in treatment. "This cultural perception of self-concept formation was recognized by the agency when developing the goal for Luke to maintain contact with his native tradition" (Hiscox & Calisch, 1998, p.62). Ferrara ends her chapter by addressing one of the most important factors when considering cultural variables, that an art therapist becomes culturally aware by actively seeking information outside of the therapy session, "I became cognizant of my responsibility to become culturally aware, learning about his lifestyle of the therapy session," and taking this approach made her "a more culturally sensitive art therapist" (p.82).

Another cultural variable to be considered in using art in the therapeutic process is that an art therapist may be working in collaboration with others who are not familiar with art therapy. Gómez Carliar and Salom (2012) wrote about their struggles with art therapy and the institution they collaborated with as they dealt with "changes in staff, chronic tardiness, lack of privacy, and difficulty in maintaining materials and space…we had to undertake a role in educating the institution about art therapy" (p.7). Chilcote (2007) also relates to this concern while doing art in Sri Lanka and working with an art therapist assistant/translator. "Topics such as privacy/ confidentiality, sensitivity towards children, tsunami trauma, and art therapy were discussed" (p.157). She also spoke about the reciprocal process. "The translator oriented me in turn to the unique cultural aspects of Sri Lankan life, such as the educational system and rituals for expressing grief" (p.157). You may be working with art therapists from different countries of origin, background, and schooling, which could also present a strain on how the art directive is delivered. Gómez Carliar and Salom (2012) reported this issue and how it became disruptive to treatment:

Instead of using supervision to focus on the children's cases, we needed its structure to come together as a treatment team while also struggling to develop common ground about the profession itself. Each intervention required an interweaving of our diverse perspectives and definitions of art therapy; each art therapist advocated for herself and for her training and background to be dominant. (p.7)

Working in collaboration with communities and institutions will be explored in more detail in later chapters. It is an important topic, and needs to be reconnoitered, as it is a principle of cultural humility that offers the art therapist guidelines towards accountability to seek diversity, inclusion, and equity.

Being aware of materials is an important variable when using art in a therapeutic setting. When working in a country outside of our country of origin there are many factors to consider. Gómez Carliar and Salom (2012) reported how the children were more interested in the "abundant and novel materials that were rich with tactile sensations" (p.7). Before presenting materials, an art therapist would benefit from making themselves familiar with the types used or native in the environment so as not to overwhelm the client or disregard the cultural impact of using unfamiliar materials. The use of expensive or acquirable materials could be welcomed, or create tension in the group between privilege and poverty. Gómez Carliar and Salom later spoke about the surprise they encountered when they asked the children what materials they wanted. "To our surprise, their list included non-traditional art supplies…array of materials they requested from their environment" (p.8).

One of the cultural variables that appears to be addressed the least is the power differential. Talwar (2010) concurs with this, as reflected in the paper "An intersectional framework for race, class, gender, and sexuality in art therapy," "From my experience in the field of art therapy, I have found that issues of difference, power and authority mostly go unacknowledged" (p.11). By a look at the media, advertising and commercials, lead actors in movies and television, one can quickly perceive which ethnic and cultural group has the power—even in our cartoons and children's shows. Yedidia and Lipschitz-Elchawi (2012) describe this in terms of "power imbalance" (p.110). When the Arab Israeli children in their study had a more positive view of the dominant group they explained it as

> the Arab Israeli children's sense of confusion regarding their sociocultural identity. Israeli Arabs are citizens of a country in which the Jewish majority rules. They are marginalized, defeated and subjected to ethnic, cultural, and social tensions…the experience and the emotional complexes created by the power imbalance between the two national groups. (pp.110–111)

Again, recognizing and shifting the power imbalance is a strong and activating principle of cultural humility. Power dynamics are at play at all times in and out of the therapeutic process; it is the art therapist's responsibility to not engage in the perpetuation of the power facilitation causing harm, derogation, or oppression within the art therapy practice, and also, as supported by Talwar (2010), "to investigate how race, class, gender, and sexuality as cultural constructs have conspired to shape subjectivity, art therapists need to examine the role of oppression, the impact of popular culture and visual media in controlling how minority populations have been viewed" (p.13). The lens imposed by society can often alter our and our client's perspectives. These ways of seeing should be examined within the therapeutic space in collaboration with the client, and addressed outside of therapy for the art therapist.

As we continue to look at the different variables in the use of art in the therapeutic process and how to address these variables in practice, ultimately, as shared by Gómez Carliar and Salom (2012), we need a safe place to explore our self-identity and culture whether inside or outside the therapeutic process: "We began to acknowledge our needs for a safe space within our own culture…" (p.7). The article continues with the writers understanding that once the immigrant begins to feel safe they can adjust and begin to "understand the host culture while simultaneously becoming more aware of his or self-identity" (p.7). Again self-identity becomes an important variable. If we look at ourselves as the immigrant into the client's country we can trust in the client as the expert and with cultural humility begin to respect and understand one another. McNiff (2009) expressed the need for further research and collaboration between cultures: "Cross-cultural dimensions of art therapy are delineated with support for further research and cooperation between cultures, with attention given to outcomes relative to art therapy practices and training" (p.101). As art therapists, if we take this into account, we could make gains in making cultural variables an instinctual part of our practice.

Currently, the use of terms such as multicultural and cross-cultural has been waning as healthcare fields are recognizing that cultural awareness needs to be more than a specialty or competence—integration into all forms of treatment. It is becoming acknowledged that all interactions are a multicultural exchange, leading to a client-centered approach. Tervalon depicts a client focus as "avoiding the 'cultural traits', practicing respectful and curious inquiry, encourage rather than obstruct the telling of the story and anticipating multiple cultural identities" (M. Tervalon, PowerPoint presentation, 2018). Being client-centered requires the understanding of privilege and permission. How often do practitioners ask for permission from those they work with, as opposed to insinuating what they want and/or need? How many assumptions are made because a therapist believes they have the privilege in all therapeutic spaces or any space in general? Whether permission is needed or given, asking conveys respect and caring. Having humility may require an art therapist to remove their wants for the client in order to hear the client convey their desires for healing to the therapist. Often, novice art therapists are challenged by their client's not wanting to create art, talk, or engage in the directive as instructed. At this time in practice, it is important to examine whether having the client engage in art at that moment is a need of the practitioner to feel competent or the client expressing a need or concern to the therapist. Asking permission also becomes effective when seeking it from our clients, but also from communities, community members, organizations, colleagues, groups, and spaces. When holding privilege, one can believe or inherently perceive oneself as having the right to be in all spaces. If seeking to address power imbalances, asking permission offers empowerment to those who may not feel empowered in spaces. Some practitioners unknowingly or knowingly refrain from asking permission out of the fear of power loss: Fear that empowering their clients, students, colleagues, or communities may reduce the power the clinician has. Some clinicians derive their self-worth from holding this power. Being culturally humble may mean being willing to make space for those who may not have a voice to be heard, even if that means conceding, nominating others, or remaining silent. Reflecting on aspects such as these can lead the art therapist to a more humble way of practicing and collaborating, as well as acknowledging cultural ramifications to the clinical, community, and therapeutic space.

Cultural awareness and self-critique can also be gained in the facilitation of the therapeutic space. Creating directives that leave room for reflection can be assessed when offering art-making to clients. Is the art therapist, through the directive, allowing the opportunity for the client to create based on their cultural lens or worldview? Or is the directive such that it guides the client to display the art therapist's biases? For example, asking the client to draw by asking "Can you share what it is like for you?" could open more opportunities for the participant to approach the directive from their own experience. Unlike asking the participant, "Can you draw what that frustration felt like," without the client disclosing that it was frustrating. Suggesting that a client draws what the clinician is assuming implies that the client must feel the same as the clinician, or may encourage the client to label a feeling, thought, or experience according to the clinician's interpretation. This becomes dangerous when the language of the client is not being honored or used. This also creates a caution for clinicians when they use their own language to label or describe a client based on assumptions.

Language can foster a prescribed way for our clients to engage and be perceived. This can come across in verbal exchange and in written sources. Clinical documentation can often illuminate a practitioner's biases, assumptions, and beliefs about a client, which then gets passed on to the next caregiver that reads it. Stigmas once written or expressed can be difficult to expunge. A statement such as "the child is slow" or even "appears to be slow" resonates differently than "the child worked slower than the other children in the class." One makes a universal description that can follow the child in all environments and activities. The other allows for the client to be observed in that particular setting without tainting how the client might engage in other areas with other undertakings. The same can be said when a therapist is writing an assessment or evaluation of a client. Often the initial description of the client, namely the "identifying information," is fraught with assumptions and biases beginning with the client's ethnicity/race, gender, or sexual orientation. Often, by how our clients present themselves, we make assumptions based on our previous experiences of societal impacts without asking the client to self-identify. Therapists can become uncomfortable with asking identity questions and instead default to what they can observe visually in the space.

When assigned a formal assessment in the Marital and Family Therapy Issues and Considerations course, I ask students to be mindful of writing the document as if the client is a subject. They are asked to include the client's own description of their presenting problem, to quote the client when documenting family history and dynamics, and to state potential cultural considerations linking them to treatment and the therapeutic relationship. When writing the dynamic formulation they are encouraged to use questioning language such as "it seems, perhaps, it may be that, etc." This is also requested throughout the document, if the student cannot specifically reference where information was gathered. Otherwise, they are asked to cite all information, as opposed to stating definitive language; for example, Ct is, Ct was, and so on. And when discussing the nature of the client relationship the students are asked to consider potential or apparent transference to the therapist, potential or apparent transference to art, potential or apparent countertransference, how countertransference may affect sessions and how the therapist will respond to countertransference. All of these aspects of writing assist the student in developing a framework that includes a culturally humble approach to viewing the client as a whole individual with whom they are engaged in an interactive experience, removing them from the "lab coat" position of assessment. There is privilege with practice; paying attention to that privilege in our tones, body language, verbal expression, and writing becomes paramount to a culturally humble practitioner.

## Understanding privilege

Privilege resides in all practitioners from all cultural backgrounds. Art therapists hold the privilege of the education and training they have obtained, as well as the personal insight gained through practice and experience. Some also have rich specialties in specific areas of research and assessment. It is important to acknowledge these distinctive skills and proficiencies. Tervalon states, "challenging power imbalances demonstrates humility by practitioners recognizing they have access to resources and knowledge and determining access to resources, knowledge, and services in the best interest of the individual" (M. Tervalon, personal communication, 2018). It is also equally essential to recognize the expertise of our clients to their own lived experience. Many of our clients have some type of knowledge of what has or will work for them, or an understanding of what their need or desire is to live a more fulfilled life. A practitioner's responsibility is to explore ways of addressing the client's concerns or guiding the client in the direction that will meet the client's goals. Having the privileges allotted to an art therapist should not supersede the client whom they work with.

Working with a client can be a challenge for both novice and seasoned practitioner. When faced with a challenged client or therapeutic engagement, a therapist may seek consultation on how to work *around* a certain perceived difficulty of a client. The privileges that the therapist holds, if not acknowledged, could prevent cultural humility from being practiced. Having the humility to ask "How do I work *with* the client" can assist the therapist and the client in working through challenges brought into the therapeutic space. Within that process of admitting not knowing, the therapeutic space becomes co-created. The therapist and the client are creating a culture together within the therapeutic engagement.

Self-reflecting and seeking consultation can be important when struggling to respond in a culturally humble way. Brems and Rasmussen (2019) share the importance of self-exploration: "a necessary and crucial approach to identifying personal biases and prejudices," and also that ongoing supervision and consultations are necessary to promote self-awareness (p.55). Having a continued art practice that offers a designated space for self-exploration can be valuable for an art therapist seeking to practice being culturally humble. When seeking cultural humility it is the therapist's personal accountability to evaluate, critique, and explore self-awareness. Therefore there is an importance in understanding one's own identity. Although this will be discussed in more detail later in this book, it is relevant to begin this dialogue when examining the practice of cultural humility within the therapeutic space.

When unfolding the attributes of a culturally humble practitioner, overall a culturally humble practitioner is genuine. Ordway (2018) shares genuine themes developed through her self-reflective research journey that may resonate with those who are on the ongoing practice to cultural humility:

> *Openness/curiosity* (in which I considered my interactions/approach in engaging in dialogues), *transparency/authenticity* (in which I considered ways that I show up in different spaces), *shame/guilt* (in which I reflected on my internal responses to different dialogues), *internalized core beliefs* (in which I considered underlining elements to my thoughts and behaviors), *self-compassion* (in which I considered correlations between self-concept and interactions with others), and *comfort* (in which I considered my response and interactions with challenges). (p.22)

Although this may not be said for everyone, building upon previous experiences and interacting in a lifelong self-reflective journey of cultural humility will foster one's own themes to developing effective attributes.

## REFLECTIVE PERSPECTIVE

### The Shape of Art Therapy Supervision by Dr. Melissa Satterberg, PhD, LMFT, ATR-BC

It is a privilege to supervise clinicians who seek to deepen their career as art therapists. My clinical training and ongoing self-assessment in my role as a supervisor, clinician, educator, and artist have been nurtured through my experiences in learning from others in both academia and clinical settings.

My contribution to the supervision process ignites my enduring passion of connection and understanding, allowing known and emergent concepts to give shape to the supervision practice. A shape, which is molded and formed from the interplay of oneself and others. I introduce the topic of cultural humility in art therapy supervision through a dialogue about the importance of being attuned to the voice and world of the client and ourselves. Diving deeper into both a verbal and art-making exchange in supervision promotes a reflective process that engages the personal biases, assumptions, and life experiences of the clinician to be exposed. This process supports ways of viewing more than the outer dimensions of the client as seen through their physical appearance, ethnicity, age, gender, and sexuality. The germination of awareness of cultural humility is indispensable through the supervision experience, with an emphasis and critical focus on all parts of the client, therapist, and the therapy encounter. The incorporation of culture is ever present with each interaction of the supervision process. The ongoing critical assessment of the art therapists' values and biases are at the crux of supervision. In group supervision, each is exposed to experiences of one another which provide a space to increase the opportunity for growth. This collaborative voice is meaningful as it encourages a broad range of knowing the whole person, the worldview of the client and the interplay between the art therapist and the client. The collective process between the dynamics of the small group enacts an enriching experience that nourishes and informs one's creative process in a clinical setting. The invitation to contribute to a larger conversation about diversity and culture lends to the potentiality of critically challenging one another, a topic that is often absent in supervisory practice. The use of cultural humility in supervisory work is essential as it bridges interactions that are communicated visually and non-verbally.

When discussing art completed in a clinical session, the visible world of what the art communicates weaves together a story that can only be truly embraced by the client and the witness (art therapist). In art therapy supervision, the experience is between the supervisor (witness) and supervisee. The action of reflecting, recognizing, and implementing changes in the therapeutic process (seen and unseen), mirrors cultural humility practice. The recognition of the power is a large aspect of the supervision and the clinical setting. As a supervisor, I strive to lead and engage supervisees in conversations about our differences, privileges, populations of clients served, and the levels of experience of the clinicians. The role of the supervisor is to educate, share knowledge of concepts and theories, and engage the learner in a dialogue. To balance the power differential, I expose vulnerability through the transparency of my experiences to enhance the reality of the interactions between others in both clinical and supervisory experiences. The role of the supervisee is to actively participate through consultation, have flexibility in communication, and commit to art-making. Knowing ourselves from the supervision process, in either role as the supervisor or supervisee, invites one to think more critically about how the therapy process evolves, considering all the intersections of diversity and power that arise in the lives of the individuals we provide service to. The ongoing, fluid, evolution of knowing oneself and others through the landscape of cultural humility allows for the shape of an experience to be developed and explored. The shape of our experience is not to be fixed or cemented into a mold. This shape, through the guidance and formulation in the supervisory relationship and the power of art-making in supervision is crucial to art therapists' professional development. Supervision allows for one's unique shape of experience to awaken perception, reflection, and attunement to the creative process. The shape of our individual understanding and experience of cultural humility is to be witnessed, honored, explored, and processed as an ongoing assessment in the practice of clinical care of others. The commitment to the practice of cultural humility is essential to the field of art therapy, reinforced through the engagement in art therapy supervision.

## RESPONSE ART

*Figure 3.2 M. Satterberg, "Evolution," 2019. Media & materials: oil pastel on ceramic tiles, 3x3 in., title: Inside Outside*

## REFLECTIVE EXERCISE C: **CREATING A PATH**

### Cultural exploration: Cycles of life

*Figure 3.3 Workshop participant, Cultural Path*

■ **Goal:** As we discuss our multidimensional and interrelated cultural identities, this exercise will assist in exploring the parts that offer a path or depiction of the whole.

■ **Materials:** White/colored paper, white/colored cardboard, collage material, color pencils, markers, pastels, a circular template.

■ **Prompt:** Cultural path exercise:

1. Begin with recollecting the aspects that make up your current identity: Going back to early family, community, individual interactions, lessons, explicit and implicit ways of knowing that began your formation of identity. Use a circular pattern to make a surface to depict identity, preferably the size of a dinner plate. Create as many circles as you feel are needed to describe all relevant aspects of self.

2. Next arrange circles according to movement, exploring what moved the circles from one path to the next. Things that can cause movement might be trauma, events, experiences, chronological child–adolescent–adult, transition in time, moving to a different country.

3. Observe whether the path is linear, cyclical, overlapping; look for themes, things that have shifted change or altered, or aspects of identity that have solidified.

# CHAPTER 4

# Cultural Humility and Community-Based Art Therapy

## *Hands: How We Connect and Reach Out to the Community—Hands-On Work*

*Figure 4.1 Collective Study Collaborator Art 004*

## Relevance of community-based art therapy

The publication *Art, Culture and the National Agenda, Strengthening Communities through Culture* (Storm, 2001), states that art and culture have long been associated with the development of America's cities and towns and the rich diversity and evolution of neighborhoods and communities. Art and culture are often used to help revitalize and improve the economies of inner cities, suburbs, and rural areas. Art and culture are also successfully used to help achieve educational goals and ameliorate some of society's most pressing problems. Although art and culture can be a source of controversy, they are more frequently a force for enhancing community identity and making communities more vibrant and prosperous. One of the cultural humility principles describes "Developing mutually beneficial partnerships with communities on behalf of individuals and defined populations," this requires the art therapist to "listen as if the speaker is wise, respecting the defining health priorities, building on existing strengths and acting as effective students of and partners with community" (Tervalon & Lewis, 2018, p.4). Progressively, the art therapist engages in, "humble and courageous self-reflection, dialogue with the community and hearing their input as expert, work with the power imbalance by distributing the knowledge and decision making often and freely, and creating 'Communities of Dialogue' to work with community members, and clients, and each other on tough issues" (Tervalon & Lewis, 2018, p.48). Most of these tasks and attributes have been echoed throughout art therapy literature and have been incorporated in community-based practices over the years (Howie, Prasad, & Kristel, 2013; Kapitan, Litell, & Torres, 2011).

Art therapy has its beginning in community-based work and art therapists have been offering community-based practices and projects for many years (Ottemiller & Awais, 2016). Lucille Venture, the first US Black female pioneer in art therapy to acquire a doctorate, exclusively focused her dissertation on art therapy and her early work in the community; she was also an original founder of the Maryland Art Therapy Association (Potash, 2005). Her thesis, "The Black beat in art therapy experiences" (1977), reflected the climate of diversity or lack thereof in the field of art therapy at that time. She began her thesis by noting that the purpose of her paper was to "introduce art therapy to a large segment of our population—a segment always underserved—minorities black, brown and white" (p.i). As Venture introduced the second and third parts of her manuscript, she strongly advocated for Black and poor communities, which were underserved populations of art therapy. She advocated for a culturally humble approach, although the concept would not be introduced until decades later. Venture noted that there was "a strong need for intellectual and philosophical viewpoint as well as practice" (pp.80–81), which reflect the understanding that "to be effective, [art therapy] must be approached in a manner which enables the poor to become actively involved, on their own terms in the struggle against racism and poverty" (p.81).

In summary of her thesis, Venture (1977) spoke to what she believed would broaden access to Black and poor communities and allow those of that community to practice in their communities. Venture challenged AATA and the field of art therapy to become less exclusive, and many steps have been taken in the field to meet this goal within AATA through the Multicultural Committee, ethics codes, and training. Although today more access is available, there still is a lack of people of color in art therapy programs (Elkins & Deaver, 2013) and of a clear approach to diversity, equity, and inclusion. Lucille is honored in her efforts to ignite changes that have improved the field and the association through her efforts.

Community-based art therapy has been defined in multiple ways within art therapy. Many terms such as "community-based participatory arts, community-based arts programming" (Bone, 2018); "participatory arts" (Hackling *et al.*, 2008); community arts studio (Howells & Zelnick, 2009); itinerant art therapy (Furman & Boeve, 2018); community-based art studios (Allen, 2008; Vick & Sexton-Radek, 2008); socially committed community art action (Timm-Bottos, 2011); social action art therapy (Golub, 2005); public practice art therapy (Timm-Bottos, 2017); group-oriented community-based expressive arts (Lynch & Chosa, 1996); and studio-based community art therapy (Nolan, 2013) have been documented. Perhaps the importance of community-based art therapy practice does not lie in the semantics of what it is labeled. Although it is imperative that an art therapist is aware of space, setting, and population, its importance is the art therapist's awareness and understanding of their approach to the space and the awareness of personal insight and the implications of their presence in the space. This also leaves room for community-based art therapy practices to exist in many spaces and be defined by those who the art therapist is in collaboration with. Along with the different terminology comes different ways of practicing and approaching community based-art therapy (Ottemiller & Awais, 2016). Whether practicing in another country, county, region, studio, gallery, or development outside an institution; with institution support, within institutional structure, or within university course work, many of these echo a cultural humility approach. This chapter will discuss specific ways cultural humility aligns with community-based art therapy and the approaches an art therapist should consider when practicing cultural humility principles. In discussing how art and culture can be a source of empowerment, we must also look at the impact of capitalism and social stress on community healing and the role of art therapy in social change; although social justice will be mentioned in a separate chapter, it is difficult to mention community without the integration of social implications.

## Effects of stress on the community and other social impacts

Capitalism leads to the division of classes, leaving the most vulnerable oppressed by those in power. Many of the most oppressed live in situations of poverty. When impoverished, stress becomes an overwhelming factor in everyday life. With lack of resources, one can become victim to crime, violence and other harmful environmental factors, leading to pathologies such as post-traumatic stress disorder and other stress-related mental illnesses. Hass-Cohen and Carr (2008) validate the need for art to combat stress pathologies in the community, addressing the stress response in the brain and summarizing, "education and successful social experience-building solutions reduce chronic stress, preserve optimal attachment functioning and encourage the longevity of health" (p.126). They encourage strength-based relationships with the community, which art therapy could impact through using art to increase a life worth living and improving the quality of life; "relationship building and creating meaning-making through the art offers some powerful strategies for mitigating the negative consequences of stress response and promoting growth" (p.126).

Joseph (2006) reverberates how oppressed communities found relief from their stress through a group mural project: "They were young to middle-aged African-American and Latino/a residents of the neighborhood, who came seeking relief from their stressful experiences... Shared grievances relating to their community's oppression became evident within the symbolic content of their murals" (p.31). Joseph foresaw the damage of capitalism and how art could be used to combat its effects on the impoverished, explaining, "I saw that capitalism was becoming more and more hegemonic, increasingly elevated in a cloud of deception, hiding its nature as a root of mass pathology. Art, I thought, could be used for unmasking this deception." Art therapy can go beyond the therapeutic office walls to impoverished communities, as Joseph shares, "art has the capacity to expose the destructive forces of self and other and make connections to the larger system" (p.31). In social action art therapy, Golub (2005) describes social action by definition as occurring in the community (p.17). She goes on, "community is many things: a classroom, hospital ward, or country. It is not a homogeneous entity but a complex network of complex individual members, including art therapists" (p.17). After Golub describes the use of social art therapy in many different countries, others share, using the model with populations and settings here in the US (Slayton, 2012). Rossetto (2012) also uses social action art therapy with community mural-making, sharing that it moves away from traditional art therapy and the traditional Western worldview. Sharing in the cultural humility principle of self-critique, she goes on to say:

Art therapists may consider how to undertake work that is aligned with a larger social and cultural purpose. Awareness of cultural paradigms and of the underlying philosophies that drive them is important, particularly for those art therapists who are working with culturally diverse populations. This awareness, in turn, may provide the opportunity to practice conscious activism through community-based therapeutic arts. (p.25)

Social action art therapy was further explored to address compassion fatigue or secondary stress amongst professionals working with domestic abuse and sexual assault clients, where the results showed a significant reduction in stress (Reim Ifrach & Miller, 2016).

Levine and Levine (2011) collaborate with the idea of using art outside our practices to elicit social change. Encouraging the growth of expressive arts, which strongly collates with art therapy, they state:

> If the field itself does not grow concurrently, it risks becoming outdated and irrelevant... Most recently this has included the field of social change... Students began to apply the work of expressive arts outside of the restricted setting of the clinic, school, or corporation to the wider world of communities and conflict-laden social groups. (p.23)

Art therapy must endorse and promote community-based art therapy as a way to move the field into the future, where community practice becomes paramount in addressing the stress and development of mental health challenges before they reach our office. Levine and Levine (2011) also encourage expressive arts to take action during times of extreme stress, which again relates directly to the profession of art therapy as changing society: "When human beings find themselves in 'dire straights' situations, the experience of the capacity for making or shaping, for taking action and feeling effective, is lost" (p.37). We see this continuously in impoverished and oppressed communities whose residents feel that there is no hope. This, the authors state, is the exact reason we should bring creative problem solving through art to those communities to practice social change. When practicing social change, we must be careful to understand our values and not impose them on others and become another form of oppression. Levine and Levine (2011) share the principles of culture humility, stating, "it is a process that required humility in how physicians bring into check the power imbalance that exists in the dynamic of physician–patient communication...requires humility to develop and maintain mutually respectful and dynamic partnerships with communities" (p.118). Meeting the needs of the community is where cultural humility emerged, as Drs. Tervalon and Murray-Garcia (1998) were asked to develop a model that would assist with the physician–patient relationship in order to address the distress and inequality that was being voiced by the community. Levine and Levine (2011) support the concept of cultural humility through the words of McNiff (1993): "the role of 'expert' should be shared through the very experience of creating and the very image that arise in the work... Follow the image. Follow the client and the community. Meet the client and community where they are" (p.47).

## Implications in practice

de Botton and Armstrong's (2013) book *Art as Therapy* addresses and questions propaganda in art, which has its earliest roots in religion and government. Because of this we often think of propaganda as negative but what if art was given an agenda to promote health in our communities? de Botton and Armstrong (2013) further address the question of creating art for more than art's sake, as another example of reaching outside our art therapy practices as they ask, "What kind of art should one make?" They assert that the "reluctance by non-artists to give guidance to and make demands on artists fatally weakens the power of art and reflects an underlying fear of addressing what art is for" (p.74). Without asking, we lose the opportunity to have our "key needs" addressed through art. They continue by suggesting, "that an agenda for art can come from outside the artist's own imagination and reflect the needs of society and the viewer's soul." Again, addressing how the practice of art therapy with the use of a collaborative community directive can be healing.

In my previous practice with youth in residential treatment I listened to the youth and their need for expression as much as possible, to develop projects that allowed them to change or affect their communities through art. For example, together with the facility's occupational therapist, someone I worked closely with, we did extravaganzas where the youth dictated the entire process, from creating the program/program pamphlets and all the creative acts in it, designing the flyer, creating the background sets, making the refreshments, and hosting. They then put on the show for the county's community, families, and care providers to showcase their talents and normalize their experience as adolescents. It also offered a necessary reprieve from their stressful relational situations. The occupational therapist and I also curated art shows/open houses in collaboration with the education department, where the youth were able to display what they had created therapeutically in day treatment, as well as their accomplishments in school, to their families and the county community.

The youth have made and donated blankets to other children who were in less desirable circumstances then their own, volunteered at senior centers to offer their time and talents to the older adults, and assisted with the Children's Fund, where they volunteered to organize and distribute toys for the children and youth in their county community for the holidays. They worked on a spring fling where they read and shared children's stories they wrote and illustrated; they presented their own digital stories and offered tours of their community garden project. The youth have also researched, designed, and constructed their own mosaic wall and created murals on their facility grounds to enhance and convey messages of hope to their community.

These projects were all done to alleviate some of the stress that has caused pathologies and damaged their attachment capabilities. Through community action and creativity they were able to learn to build relationships, share traumas, and express repressed emotions appropriately. Giving the youth the opportunity to take ownership of these activities allowed freedom from oppression, which is constant in the child welfare system. An agenda was provided to them, giving them the responsibility to create for a greater purpose beyond themselves, in the hope that their reflections would be shared with someone in a similar situation, allowing the art to heal in them, others, and their communities.

When looking at the youth population as well as other community groups or spaces, a culturally humble art therapist must remain aware and refrain from focusing on the perceived detriment and the outsiders defined meanings of the population's behavior. It can be easy to make assumptions of what we think is useful for a particular group in becoming an empowered community, based on our own biases and beliefs. Slayton (2012) cautions against and reflects on assuming the needs of a community in sharing accounts of what was assumed to be required to be an effective art therapist and discovering the benefits of listening to the client, sharing:

> The powerful watching, listening, and not having to say anything that goes along with being an art therapist conveys genuine acceptance to the adolescent client. It also allows the art therapist the time and space to genuinely care about what is being watched. My questions about what the adolescents needed (whether supplies, limits, or support) were heard as expressions of care and attention. The group became a mutual exchange of respectful interactions—a community building a community—with the art product as the container for both the said and the unsaid. (p.184)

## Community-based art therapy in education training

As community-based art therapy has been expressed as effective in practice it has become paramount in the educational training of art therapists. In preparation for professional practice, students are given practicum experiences, often in community settings, as their first introduction into becoming clinicians in the field. Having experiences in this area of practice becomes crucial in the development of skill and awareness. Implementing cultural humility principles integrated with experiential learning can impact both identity and facilitation of a novice art therapist. Kapitan (2012) gives an example where engaging in an international learning experience caused a student to face her assumptions. Kapitan echoes the words of Bain in sharing, "A good learning experience places students in a situation where, despite their deep desires, their existing mental models simply will not work" (p.148). Through the support of supervision, the student was able to develop the "capacity for handling not only the cultural differences but also the emotional trauma that sometimes accompanies cognitive dissonance or challenges to students' beliefs" (p.148). In the next chapter, assumptions, biases, and beliefs will be examined, as they are at the core of critically self-reflecting in cultural humility and echoed throughout this book. As a hands-on engagement, community exposure can offer a challenge to our assumptions; biases and beliefs, indicated in Kapitan as she recalls her student's experience, "people who develop mental and technical flexibility are able to recognize their assumptions and shift expectations and approaches to fit the situation at hand" (p.148).

As a full-time assistant professor at Loyola Marymount University (LMU), I have had many of my own engagements with art therapy training and community-based models. Many were put in place by the previous chair, Linesch (Linesch & Carnay, 2005; Linesch, Metzl, & Treviño, 2015), who shares the development of the training program in San Miguel de Allende, Mexico. Along with this, which has become an ongoing and currently integrated aspect of the Master's program, Linesch also modeled the developed and ongoing service learning components, such as students being immersed in Dolores Mission School with the early support of Father Greg Boyle, as part of their Child Psychotherapy course and another experience in Center Juvenile Hall for their Adolescent Psychotherapy course. I have had the pleasure of teaching both of these courses over the years and, through using cultural humility principles as an assessment into their learning experience, students have reported that the integration of these visits as a way to conceptualize and develop awareness into these populations has been invaluable.

Related to the previous chapter, both of these community-based learning courses were assessed to enhance the academic dimension of existing outreach programs and for the development of new community-based learning courses with a faith and justice component. At the onset of this implemented assessment, a new syllabus was created to encompass components of cultural humility, which incorporates the principles of faith and justice. Within the syllabi, new student outcomes, community-based art engagements, reflective projects, and assessments were added. The assessment included two components: a 39-item inventory that offers the students a chance to reflect on their assumptions, biases, and beliefs; and an art journal drawing depicting their understanding of engaging in a community with cultural humility. The assessment was created to offer an effective depiction of the overall strength of the attention paid to cultural humility in both community-based learning courses, which address the faith and justice aspects of this grant.

In conjunction with this effort, the first action step was to modify the Self Identity Inventory (SII), a six-scale, 72-item inventory to assess the students' thinking patterns and how they identify themselves prior to their engagement in the class and after engaging in class psycho-education, collective art, individual reflective art, and the community-based work. The assessment was modified into a 39-item inventory, maintaining the six-scale ratio so as to not alter the key scoring of the assessment. At the beginning of the semester students are given a link and asked to complete the Self Identity Inventory Altered (SIIa) prior to attending the Child Psychotherapy course. The students are also asked, prior to the Child Psychotherapy course, to create an image depicting their "concept of engaging in a community with cultural humility." They are asked to bring the depiction to the first day of class, where they attach their drawing to a journal, leaving the opposite page blank. At the end of the semester, the students are asked to complete another drawing depicting their "concept of engaging in a community with cultural humility." This drawing is placed on the opposite page to their first drawing and analyzed to assess their increased awareness of engaging in the community with cultural humility. It was observed that many students began with a narrow, growing, and individualized understanding of cultural humility. At the end of the class students' reflections covered the page with images that depicted expansion, interrelatedness, and awareness.

To assist the students in developing awareness, they engage in an academic lecture course given by the writer and by guest lecturers who are doing work with populations in community settings; they are assigned literature readings that address doing art therapy in community-based settings; and they write reflections and art responses based on their experiences in the class and assigned readings. Finally, it is arranged with community leaders for students to participate in community engagements using art during both the Child Psychotherapy and Adolescent Psychotherapy courses.

Within these community engagements I take time to meet with administrators, guards, staff, teachers, class aides, and so on to continue forming mutual relationships with the communities. The students also follow this modeling and interact respectfully with each community member. These community engagements again appear to be effective in offering examples to the students when it comes to clinical/theoretical learning by having actual artwork and engagement of the community populations, offering a depiction of the theories and themes learned in the courses. Recently, after developing a relationship with the university's director of community-based learning service and action, as a research mentor, I led my research group in a community-based art therapy experience to offer a hands-on approach to developing, facilitating, and assessing a community-based art therapy project. All the students had based their research on different aspects of community-based art therapy practices, most choosing a self-exploration into a culturally humble approach to this area of work. I modeled the development, implementation, and assessment of a community-based art therapy project. The students came with me to meet with LMU's Director of Community-Based Learning Service and Action, and three different community organizations. They supported me while I explained our program, the students' research, and what we could offer as pre-licensed students and licensed professionals. The students reported being inspired as I spoke with confidence about the validity of the profession in this group setting. We were contacted later by one of the organizations and together began the collaborative process of developing and implementing a community project. The students were actively involved and witnessed both the challenges and strengths of doing community work as well as the culturally humble approach that is needed to carry it out.

The students eventually facilitated a two-day art engagement group with the assistance of an art therapy research mentor, myself, for mothers and children who were victims of domestic violence, at a domestic violence center. A brief pre- and post-evaluation was offered and given to the community-based organization's (CBO) program coordinator to use to assess the value of the art experience with the population. Although the students expressed gratitude for being part of the experience from beginning to end, they also struggled with having such a brief time with the community. In the end, I believe they found it rewarding and it also increased their awareness of self and others, related to the principles of cultural humility.

As expressed by Furman and Boeve (2018), working closely with the community outreach coordinator to plan and co-facilitate a focused intervention allows students increased autonomy and a more parallel relationship with the experienced art therapist, both of which can contribute to the evolution of professional identity. Further, exposure to a diversity of clients and therapeutic approaches offers graduate students an invaluable opportunity to explore their emerging professional identity, while understanding the reciprocal impact on the community they serve. Short-term community outreach therapy provides students with the benefit of exposure to an alternative treatment model with a focus on engagement of clients, rather than identification of pathology (Elmendorf, 2010; Lambert *et al.*, 2001). In her own words, before engaging in the community-based project, a student expressed:

> The data was based on my thoughts, feelings, and experiences that surfaced both through consistent self-reflection and through my work with a community-based art therapy engagement at a domestic violence shelter. This engagement was the result of a collaboration between my research mentor, my research colleagues, and representatives/advocates from the shelter, and was designed to utilize art therapy to help support a group of women and their children, who live at the shelter. Two art therapy groups were created (one for the mothers, one for the children), which took place two times over two weeks, at their home. My engagement with the initial, preparatory process (collaborative meetings, scheduling, the design of the engagement), as well as with the art therapy groups themselves (in which I co-facilitated the mother's group with a research colleague, with assistance from my research mentor), informed my data, and will be discussed in conjunction with my personal inner

workings. Privilege also became a central focus in considering my role in my upcoming community engagement with the domestic violence shelter. I journaled about feeling nervous, due to the fact that I believe privilege is designed to be invisible to those who hold it, which I correlated to an assumed ignorance on my part. I discussed feeling fearful that my ignorance might affect my ability to be culturally humble in a way that might be damaging to the women I was intending to support. I also felt apprehensive to undertake a leadership role of co-facilitator, because I wanted to center the experiences of the women and did not want to assume what they needed. (Ordway, 2018, pp.24–25)

Following the engagement, the same student shared, in her discussion of her research:

This, in conjunction with my experience in working with the domestic violence shelter, has felt like an important step in understanding and practicing ways in which I can best support communities through the use of art therapy in my future work. As this research has illuminated the commonalities and discrepancies between theory and practice, I feel that my next step is to continue to strengthen my practice through authentic engagement with community work. This intent is in direct correlation with my original research question (*how can I utilize the culmination of my social justice education/awareness to inform my engagement with community art therapy to enhance cultural humility?*), of which my theme-informed response at this point in time is: By exerting the most effort I can/trying my best, by authentically listening to the views and needs of others openly, by holding myself accountable through the lens of self-compassion rather than shame/guilt, and by continuously challenging my own areas of comfort. (Ordway, 2018, pp.24–25)

After engaging in the community-based project, many of the students expressed their challenges with engaging so briefly with the community. They described wanting to stay engaged and do more, while understanding why the limitations were in place. Initially, we had planned to spend twice as much time as we did; unfortunately, there were scheduling challenges due to many factors related to all parties involved, including the university and the community-based organization. Labeled as "community-based itinerant art therapy," Furman and Boeve (2018) share the benefits of this educational model:

> [It] provides a valuable opportunity to provide a high-quality intervention to empower and support underserved populations in the context of their own communities... Bringing services into the community can help dispel fears about participating in therapy by offering direct experience... Taking services on the road, students and experienced clinicians alike have an opportunity to join clients in their individual, cultural, and historical context outside of a traditional therapy setting... For community outreach, short-term art therapy groups can be practical and effective, leaving a powerful impression on both the participating students and the clients. (pp.65–66)

Although brief, these community-based experiences have had a long-lasting impact on the students and the communities. The students appeared both invigorated and frustrated by the experience. They spoke about how honored they felt that the participants shared so much with them and that it was a transformative occurrence. They also spoke about the challenges and the flexibility needed to engage in community-based work, while reflecting on the want and the need to do more. They asked about engaging in more similar community-based art therapy projects and one student, in particular, volunteered her time in a future endeavor, which will be discussed later in this chapter.

In this particular engagement, the participants expressed how much they enjoyed the experience and looked forward to engaging in art that way again. It appeared that it gave them some relief from the regularly scheduled activities and obligations. Expecting to find depictions of the challenges these women were dealing with, we instead witness images of positive self-reflection, future goals, and aspirations. Some of the participants simply created a collage of things they enjoyed and places that brought them peace. And again, supporting the decrease of stress in the community, Furman and Boeve state, "Short-term art therapy groups can be creative and flexible, reducing stress for both clients and clinicians" and "short-term group therapy can provide an inexpensive and flexible way to meet the varied needs of clients in the community by reducing stress, anxiety, and even depression" (2018, p.66).

In addition, Furman and Boeve (2018) share attributes needed for itinerant providers, also needed for all community-based art therapy work and the integration of a culturally humble approach of self-awareness, working mutually for the benefit of the community and developing institutional accountability: "Itinerant providers are able to work with clients who may have less access to therapeutic services, and who may avoid seeking help due to social stigma, fear of emotional flooding, and resistance to self-disclosure" (p.65). Community-based art engagements not only also offer the individual to come into spaces bringing materials; they also offer a temporary space to engage intimately with the facilitators and the creative process. If structured in a way that changes the dynamic of a familiar space, such as rearranging furniture, working from an opposite side of a room, or simply referring to the space by another name, the participants can feel the safety of their environment while developing a new cultural space. Furman and Boeve refer to this: "The mobile art therapist has a unique skill set to generate a temporary secure space where participants may engage in creativity and self-exploration (Kalmanowitz & Lloyd, 2002) through strengths-based group art interventions that move from the individual experience to make connections with the community" (p.65). As this cultural space is co-created, the art therapist must have an understanding of their implication on the space and an awareness of their cultural aspects that may impact the experience for both the community and the facilitators involved. Furman and Boeve (2018) share that

> Community-based itinerant therapy requires that clinicians be adequately informed, mindful, and adaptive to the client's cultural context... In addition to clinical training, therapists working in the community must develop awareness of how their own cultural identity and prejudices might impact their work and relationships to others (Ottermiller & Awais, 2016). (pp.65–66)

Again, being culturally humble and reflecting on one's biases, assumptions, and beliefs about the communities they engage with is paramount. Going into communities should be done in the service of the community, not for the feeling of altruism for the art therapist.

Some of the research students began their studies by exploring the definition of community-based art therapy. Feen-Calligan, Moreno, and Buzzard (2018) defined service learning and community-based research, justifying the importance of both in art therapy education, addressing the importance of assessing both students and community-based organizations for effectiveness and need: "With growing trends in community-based art therapy practice, greater attention to the community agencies where art therapists work is necessary and valuable to art therapy preparation" (p.1). The article "describes new frontiers in community-based art therapy practice and education utilizing critical service-learning to nurture partnerships between art therapy educational programs and community centers and agencies, which has resulted in increased knowledge about community (partner) needs" (p.2). Having worked with a variety of communities over the years, implementing art therapy practices in these settings presents its own challenges. One of these challenges is to not assume the needs or the desires of the community group. In my own experience, I was challenged by a community partner when they expressed feeling co-opted after I agreed to present the project at a conference, assuming that the partner would like to be present for the workshop but not consulted in the development of the presentation. My own humility felt put on trial as I had to examine my need to work without the scheduling challenges of working with the community partner. We had been in collaboration from the onset of her seeking me out and proposing a collective project. We met and designed the project with expectations discussed prior to and during the community engagement. We had not clearly discussed what would happen after until our debriefing, which had to be pushed out months after the closing of the project due to both of our schedules. Within that time I was approached and asked to quickly decide on presenting the project at an upcoming conference. I very much wanted the community partner to engage and believed I was being charitable by handling the administrative work and decisions. Furman and Boeve (2018) speak about additional challenges such as working within the existing program structure; being mindful of the perceived power differential; possible resistance to new programming by community organizations; the clarification of responsibilities prior to the first visit; specific requirements by the community-based organization; ensuring a safe space for facilitation; approval and transportation of materials; advance and thorough knowledge of the population; the therapist feeling the pressure to make a difference quickly, possibly leading to rushing the therapeutic process; most importantly, it may not be suitable for all populations (pp.66–67).

## Community-based art therapy work and implications for specific populations

Potash *et al.* (2017) mention cultural humility in regard to ethical implications of cross-cultural international art therapy in first reverberating cultural competence in defining the importance of self-awareness, knowledge, and skills, then expressing the words of Hook *et al.* (2013): "Cultural humility, on the other hand, emphasizes 'an interpersonal stance that is other-oriented rather than self-focused, characterized by respect and lack of superiority toward an individual's cultural background and experience'"(p.76). Potash *et al.* goes on to offer the installation of cultural humility in foreign countries: "Preparing to work from a culturally humble, decolonizing framework requires learning about the historical, political, economic, and structural legacies of colonialism and White supremacy" (p.76). I believe this can be transferred into all populations and communities. Holding, having openness, establishing and building collaborative relationships, honoring "stakeholders," and assessing motivations become the foundations of engaging communities as a culturally humble practitioner/collaborator (Potash *et al.*, 2017).

Challenges of working in communities with special populations are captured by Fobear (2017), who explores dilemmas of community art with LGBT refugees, explicitly naming the responsibility to listen to marginalized voices in order to bear witness and reveal power structures that create a space for the interrogation of power structures. Fobear states that "power imbalances are always present, even if the participants are eager and willing to share their stories with a journalist, artist, or researcher. There is a privilege in asking for a person's story" (p.54), again aligns the cultural humility practice of seeking to equalize power imbalances and not impeding the client's story. As in my cultural humility training with Dr. Melanie Tervalon, Fobear shares Chimamande Adichie's 2009 TED talk, where she speaks about the danger of the single story:

> Allowing one story to represent the multitude of complex human experiences produces another form of violence for marginalized communities by removing them from a position of authority based on lived experience and knowledge, instead making them passive objects for consumption by outsiders. (Adichie, 2009, p.55)

Through the years I have found passion in community-based art therapy. Witnessing the stories shared by these communities and the individuals who convey their interrelated roles in their communities has been life-changing, as they consistently guide and adjust my practice of cultural humility. Two recent exposures have not just enlightened me about the communities and the practice of community-based art therapy, they have also brought awareness to me, as each offered an examination into my assumptions, biases, and beliefs. On both occasions, I was fortunate to work with teams of art therapists that unselfishly offered themselves to all aspects of facilitation and displayed the practice of cultural humility in their own walk, awareness, and skill set.

Recently, I had the privilege of leading a team of art therapists in facilitating a week-long, after-school art therapy experience for high school youth in combination with a dialectical behavioral therapy (DBT) curriculum; the program was sponsored by a public schools organization at the community health school in what is considered a low socioeconomic area of the city. I and another part-time faculty worked closely with the Director of Programs, who initially came to us seeking creative emotional support for the students she works with. Together we created a curriculum and incorporated developed outcomes produced by the CBO and objectives developed by my partner and I. As the "community outreach coordinator," I reached out to our alumni and from a group of interested individuals chose a team with strong capabilities to work with this community (Furman & Boeve, 2018, p.67). Together with this team, we developed the week's planning, incorporating a daily focus on a DBT module and skills, together with step-by-step art instructions for the final piece. The challenge in this project was scheduling the closing presentation. With collaboration, we were able to come up with an alternative, which proved to be valuable to both the team and students, according to their post-evaluation feedback.

This project explored approaching, creating, and facilitating a community art-based project using the principles of cultural humility and DBT. Through engaging in the project students were offered an art directive and were psycho-educated on the DBT modules and skills to engage in self-identity, cultural aspects of self, and stress management skills. The art directive and project encouraged the team as practitioners to practice within the community and offer practical approaches to collaborating with CBOs to effectively design a curriculum for the healing treatment of clients. The importance of this project was that it could be used with a multitude of populations and settings; although some individuals may have dexterity and motor skill challenges, the directive could be altered to assist many. Because of the resourcefulness and mobility of materials used in this project, the directive and skill-building could be used in many clinical and non-clinical settings.

Over the past summers, I was invited to participate in a creative camp that unites children to heal relationships with their mothers in federal prison. This program provides a rare opportunity for the child of a mother in prison to create and reinforce sustainable family bonds, as well as to nurture the concept of being part of a family unit. It is a meaningful week-long summer program for children to heal and reconnect with their incarcerated mothers by creating art together. Utilizing a trauma-informed approach to art therapy and family support, professionals facilitate fun and educational activities aimed at building stronger relationships. The experience was transformative for me as I witnessed intense and intimate family relationships that began as estranged and ended solidified. Being inside the prison system and meeting the women was illuminating, as it was apparent that they were mothers like most others, wanting to be supportive and close with their children. I appreciated and felt honored to engage in this experience as I once again had the privilege to work with the same part-time faculty from the previous project, along with LMU alumni. I was humbled by the mothers' acceptance of us, as they trusted us to guide them through the week with their children. We were open in conveying our privilege and thanked the mothers for allowing us into their space. In return they appeared to respect our counsel and experience as they engaged in the art-making process, sharing activities and cherished moments with their children. Integration into the facility became important as we developed relationships with the prison guard and activities coordinator. We were also tasked with collaborating with the non-profit center that organized this camp—an organization with their own expectations and ethics. This became complicated when the center wanted to bring cameras and reporters into the sessions with the mothers and children. Although we understood their need for exposure to secure funding, we were especially cognizant to adhere to our art therapist ethical codes in protecting the community from harm. Trying to compromise these two positions became challenging as the dynamics between the three entities (art therapists, prison officials, and non-profit) became estranged. It became difficult to repair this, as things became more convoluted and miscommunication continued to occur. This appeared to impact our team in exercising a culturally humble approach. Working hard to practice being humble, we stayed present with the community while consulting with each other about the outside environmental strains. In the end, what was most important was the community we were directly serving, while also not demonizing those we were in collaboration with. Understanding all positions became paramount, most importantly, recognizing that, regardless of circumstance and space, we were in the presence of families and our task at hand was to create an environment for healthy attachment and supportive community. Keeping this cultural humble stance wherever services are provided may offer a mutually beneficial and client-centered experience in the many settings art therapists work.

The goal is to provide service to the community before the implications of stress in their environment become pathologized in the members of that community and a member arrives in our institutionalized settings, where they are diagnosed and labeled, then given treatment we assess as most useful. Sajnani, Marxen, and Zarate (2017), note the relevance of giving space to the client to explore without labels, similar to our offered art engagement at the prison. The role of a culturally humble art therapist is to be a guide to the client, who is the expert of their lived experience; allowing the women to be mothers and the children to be cared for as children was instrumental in this project, as "Those who are seen as Other are often subject to dehumanizing, criminalizing narratives which are used to promote fear" (Sajnani *et al.*, 2017, p.28). As shared by Sajnani *et al.*, we had little concern for the product of the art; we allowed the community to engage how they felt inclined:

> From their very conception, the spaces should be freed from any instrumentalization of the arts, whether this is of a capitalistic or institutional nature: publicity and accumulation of symbolic capital for/of the sponsor in the former case or a public acknowledgment of the institution in the latter. Both usually follow a capitalist logic in the form of the over-valuation of the final, tangible result, as well as its fossilization. (p.29)

We were there to guide a facilitation as opposed to offering therapy.

> In art therapy, the institutional discourses of the art and therapy fields come together. Art therapists need to undertake a critical analysis of both so as to avoid the unchallenged influence of hegemonic discourses concerning the making and perception of art, as well as the dominant discourse of psychopathology. (Sajnani *et al.*, p.30)

The practice of community-based art therapy with cultural humility principles must incorporate the person's lived experiences: "contending with a person's personal history, it is important to consider how social, economic, and/or political violence in the form of racism, homophobia, or poverty, for example, contributes to expressions of distress in the form of anxiety or otherwise" (pp.34–35). The goal of the culturally humble art therapist is to create a space that is empowering, offering the opportunity for temporary relief from stress for communities with low resources, where they can experience freedom, resistance, experimentation, and empowerment (p.30). While co-constructing their lived experiences and realities "participants can feel accepted and comfortable enough to create their narratives in order to deconstruct institutionalized lives and situations of domination" (p.30). The art therapist is there to offer agency and advocacy with a person-centered approach. The communities, in turn, become the expert, using their innate qualities of strength and resilience to foster a new space with hope and growth.

To develop these collaborative community relationships and experience, an art therapist must show belief and passion in their field and be willing to speak about it in many spaces, making efforts to meet others and display a motivation and drive for equity. Culturally, our hands are used in many different ways in many different communities to communicate with others. We use hands as a form of speech, to express greetings, welcome, impediment, discontent, gratitude, and the list goes on. Within art therapy practice, included in those ways are the ways we offer support through connection and the handling of materials. This can be done directly in the art-making process, sometimes referred to as the "third hand" (Kramer, 1986). This culturally humble approach to reaching out, joining, offering a hand, taking things at hand, connecting, working *with*, learning from each other, can move community-based art therapy to an approach that becomes embedded in the field related to education, practice, theory, research, and publishing.

## REFLECTIVE PERSPECTIVE

### Art Therapy, Cultural Competency, and Domestic Violence Survivors by Angela Parker

For the past 12 years, I have worked with women, men, and children who are victims of domestic violence (DV). I have seen these survivors struggle to rebuild their lives and try to make sense of what has happened to them. It is a daunting task that is neither easy nor linear, and oftentimes, "traditional service models," while well intentioned, do not work.

Domestic violence wreaks havoc on the mind, body, and soul. One in every three women in the United States has been beaten, coerced into sex, or otherwise abused during her lifetime (Black *et al.*, 2011), while one in seven men will experience severe physical violence by an intimate partner in their lifetime (Centers for Disease Control and Prevention, 2018). According the National Center for Children Exposed to Violence, up to 10 million children witness some form of DV annually. Frequently, the abuser is a member of their own family (Black *et al.*, 2011). It should be no surprise to anyone that African American women experience DV at a rate that is disproportionately higher than their Anglo American counterparts (Bent-Goodley, 2001; Hampton, Oliver, & Magarian, 2003; Nicolaidis *et al.*, 2010). African American women also have a DV homicide rate that is four times higher than their Anglo American counterparts (Hampton *et al.*, 2003).

It is now widely accepted that victims of DV often struggle with mental health issues as a result of the abuse. Research shows that DV survivors tend to suffer from post-traumatic stress disorder (PTSD), an anxiety disorder that is characterized by flashbacks, avoidance, depression, and hypersensitivity (Schouten *et al.*, 2014). However, African American women who are victims of DV have historically had their mental health needs ignored (Bethea-Whitfield, Harley, & Dillard, 2005). This is important because, as Carey (2006) points out, "trauma often involves and resides in the body" (p.10). African American women who are victims of DV must also not only unpack the trauma of their abuse, but must face the toll that experiencing a lifetime of racism and sexism has taken on their choices and self-image (Thompson *et al.*, 2000).

As someone who works at one of the only DV programs created to serve the specific needs of African American women, I have always understood the importance of utilizing culturally grounded approaches when offering services to victims of trauma. Researchers define cultural competency as the incorporation of cultural knowledge, norms, and values of a specific culture into services in ways that acknowledge and meet their culturally unique needs (Betancourt *et al.*, 2003; Sue, 2001). While cultural competency hinges on understanding the psyche of a person, it can be actualized only if those who provide services to individuals implement this knowledge into their programs and services to eliminate what Donnelly *et al.* (2005) referred to as the *othering* of African American women. In this way, you create safe spaces for African American women in which they are not viewed as an *other* and where they have the autonomy for self-definition and self-empowerment (Collins, 2002).

Historically, visual art has been used to make sense of pain (Malchiodi, 1997) and visual art therapy offers a unique approach for working with those with PTSD (Avrahami, 2006). While I believe that words are the most powerful tool we have in our arsenal to tell our story, for those who have been stripped of their power to verbally express their pain for months, even years, the words may no longer come. Research shows that many with PTSD have a hard time utilizing verbal cues to express their trauma (Van der Kolk, 1994; Van der Kolk & Fisler, 1995). It is in that moment that art can become a lifeline. It has been my experience, that it is through the visual expression of their experiences that clients find the language to communicate their trauma (Avrahami, 2006).

Therapy, even art therapy, tends to be a controversial subject for African American women because African American women have been taught to be strong no matter the circumstances (Bent-Goodley, 2001) and to view therapy as a weakness that other people indulge in (Bethea-Whitfield *et al.*, 2005). They often see little value in therapy because they have been taught to see little value in their own well-being. Also, when they do decide to seek help, they tend to face many barriers to therapy, including access to culturally relevant services (Bethea-Whitfield *et al.*, 2005).

In an attempt to embrace new models for mental health, my organization has incorporated art into our clients' healing process for more than a decade. Of all the programs that we offer, I have found that our clients love our "Healing through the Arts" offerings the best and revel in the opportunity to use painting, collaging, and photography as a way to express their pain.

A few years ago we hosted an art therapy session with an actual marriage and family therapist, Dr. Louvenia Jackson. It was a revelation. I realized that if we were really going to utilize art as a healing tool, then we needed to incorporate trained counselors who used purposeful and methodical methods to treat complex psychosocial disorders that were beyond the scope of our volunteer art teachers' abilities.

The integration of a therapeutic component to our art projects transformed the program. The art projects became more intentional and the dialogue around the finished product richer and more self-reflective. It also seemed to me that for the clients, it made a difference to see this young, Black woman who looked like them *making it okay* for them to express themselves. Consequently, rather than just act as a stress reliever, the art projects were now a four-dimensional therapeutic experience. It seemed to me that through the art project the clients were having a type of out of body experience where they were able to remove themselves from the hurt of past traumatic events and create images of themselves that were rooted in power, instead of pain. They were able to create their own vision of themselves—they could literally change how they saw themselves in their world.

During the session, clients who were naturally closed off became more open and more relaxed. One client in particular, a young, slender girl with red boxed braids, was initially having a hard time concentrating, her eyes darting repeatedly to the childcare room where her three very young and rambunctious children were often heard laughing, crying, or yelling. As the session continued, and she began to understand the nature and purpose of the project, I saw how she began to center herself in the room, and allow herself to be present, and, as she became connected to the project, the hands she used to feed, hold, and change her babies were now feverishly being used as a mechanism to help her literally look at her own pain.

When working with clients I have adopted the physician's mantra of "do no harm" because I believe that physical and emotional healthcare is interlinked. It amazes me how art therapy allows us to gently take our clients by the hand and give them the breadth and space they need to define their own narrative in a way that is not intrusive or inauthentic. It is a "treatment" in which the recipient gladly complies with no fear.

Anyone who works with trauma survivors knows that trauma leaves victims feeling out of control, and, in art, specifically art that incorporates cultural norms and values, the artist is in control of most of the act—from which tools to use, to how the images are shaped, and what colors and textures should be incorporated. Order replaces chaos and the healing can finally begin.

Angela N. Parker is the Director of Training and Programs at Jenesse Center, Inc. Dr. Parker is the Executive Director of Phenom Girls, a non-profit that mentors at-risk middle school girls. She is the editor and publisher of *GeneratioNext*, an online newsmagazine that focuses on youth-centric stories, and *Nspire*, an online newsmagazine that spotlights the positive work people and organizations are doing in their community. She also manages *Like the Sun and the Moon*, an online hub that focuses on topics related to Black women and girls. She is the author of *Tethered*, *The Yellow Pages*, *The Specter of War*, and *Nia Ever After*. She received her BA from UCLA, her MA from National University, and her EdD from USC.

## RESPONSE ART

*Figure 4.2 Domestic violence center art therapy research project participant artwork. Artwork presents many layers of self, family, and connection to community*

# REFLECTIVE EXERCISE D: **HOW DOES YOUR PATH INTERSECT/INTERACT OR ENGAGE WITH OTHERS'? (***CULTURAL FABRICS OF SELF, INTIMATE OTHERS, & COMMUNITY***; JACKSON & METZL, 2017)**

■ **Goal:** To examine the ways we relate to others and ourselves; how we are informed by both our personal and collective experiences. Using fabric removes the representational aspects to encourage a more authentic way of engaging for all creative levels and abilities.

■ **Materials:** Variety of fabric materials, fabric glue, fabric markers, sharpies, needle and thread, glitter, glitter glue, sequins, buttons, pipe cleaners, found objects for embellishments.

■ **Prompt:**

1. Create an image related to "How do you see yourself?"

   As you create, reflect then add to that piece "In what ways do you relate to others (parts of self, aspects of identity)?"

2. Take the "self" piece and place your image of self within the context of intimate others (family, partner, social group, etc.).

   Reflect on the important collective experiences and collective knowing that you are a part of (family, friends, groups, communities), which has impacted your identity?

3. Take the "self and other" art piece and place your image in relation to community.

   Reflect on the ways in which we are informed by and apply our personal and collective knowing.

# CHAPTER 5

# Cultural Humility and Art Therapy: Approaches to Social Justice

*Heart: Braveheart, Compassion, Heart of Gold—Strong and Empowering*

*Figure 5.1 Having compassion, holding the frustration with loving hands, Collective Study Collaborator Art 003*

## Diversity, equity, and inclusion

Studying diversity is not just a matter of learning about people's cultures, values, and ways of being; it involves discovering how multiple factors underline the fundamental axes of societies, institutional systems, social issues, and the possibility of social change (Calisch, 2003). The study and the use of multicultural training also have to do with the practitioner's own self-knowledge of his or her own culture and self-identity. Cultural humility begins with having knowledge and awareness of "the ground on which we stand," making note of social and political movements including civil rights, immigration, diversity and destiny (Tervalon & Lewis, 2018). When looking at the history of the United States, it is important to look at the founding principles and who developed them, who was included and who was omitted. Examining this country's structure can illuminate the dynamics that fostered oppression, colonialism, and, in some cases, annihilation and eradication. Because our founding principles were not written to reflect the rights of all humans inhabiting the country and how they manifested in the make-up of our country, crucial movements were organized like the united farm workers, civil rights, the national organization for women, and LGBTQIA rights movements to name a few. Because of these movements, amendments were made to the Constitution and the Civil Rights Act was passed. Although these changes represent some progress, injustices and societal "isms" still exist, sparking further and current movements. Developing from a charged social event, namely the Rodney King beating and riots, cultural humility has its foundations in social justice and change. At its core, adapting cultural humility into art therapy becomes a natural transition, as social justice has become a major emphasis of the art therapy movement, philosophy, theory, and practice. To begin exploring social justice and its relationship to practice, cultural humility directs us to define and have awareness of words we use, such as race, power, privilege, culture, "isms," and the term humility itself.

Having a cultural humble stance does not insinuate complacency or passivity, nor is it its opposite; arrogance. Arrogance defined is "an insulting way of thinking or behaving that comes from believing that you are better, smarter, or more important than other people"

(Merriam-Webster, 2019a). Humility is "marked by modesty in behavior, attitude or spirit; showing patience, gentleness, and moderation about one's own abilities and values." It is "not arrogant or prideful, which in the context of the original article meant curbing the physicians' drive towards being all right and all-knowing in all areas of all things!" (Tervalon, 2012). As summarized by this quote by C Joybell C, "Be careful not to mistake insecurity and inadequacy for humility! Humility has nothing to do with the insecure and inadequate! Just like arrogance has nothing to do with greatness!" Having cultural humility requires one to stand for what is just and take a stance for equity by advocating through dialogue with others and actively engaging in critical self-examination.

Talwar (2019) offers a comprehensive perspective of "Why Social Justice?": "a social justice paradigm focuses on community building, empowerment, sustainability, equity, and justice in a domestic and international context. It expands the vision of art therapy" (p.11). When an art therapist takes an active role in social justice, it is imperative for that therapist to ask themselves what their motivation is and in what ways they are asserting their privilege. I have been approached by white art therapists asking for advice on how to show groups of non-white clients that they are one of them and that they want to help. I respond by asking the art therapist, "Is this a need of the client or the need of the therapist?" There is a relevance to recognizing that for some art therapists they are not "one of them," and in that recognition they may be able to become a stronger ally and advocate by witnessing, listening, and using their privilege to meet the stated needs of the group. Activating and repairing a space may mean asking the community what they need, even if the cost removes or recedes the therapist from the equation. Stepping back may be a way to encourage space for solutions to develop. These acts of advocacy can assist in decolonizing or dismantling established dominance, balancing the power imbalance required in cultural humility. Talwar also shares how decolonizing has been called on and discussed by some art therapists (p.11).

After offering a historical overview of psychiatry and important Supreme Court rulings, Talwar (2019) looks at the mental health system and the location of art therapy. Moving in social justice with cultural humility is about maintaining being reflective and thoughtful while also being assertive. Understanding the social structures and dynamics, then assessing your role in those systems, is critical. Talwar states, "The precursors of art therapy directly relate to the intellectual and sociological developments of the late nineteenth and early twentieth century" (p.30), so having this historical context and a comprehension of the art therapist's current implications to all systems is also crucial. Art therapists must pay attention to where their efforts are being incited and have the responsibility to pursue and address that provocation. Talwar goes on to convey that the early development of our societal structures in our formations, including art therapy, has marginalized groups of individuals and "undoing the damage caused by the eugenics ideology required several social movements" (p.33). When involved in those movements, understanding that movements are just that, fluid, as in cultural humility. The point of the movement is to cause change in order to transcend. Having apprehension of this transcendence recognizes that not everyone comprehends a cultural humble approach. For some, it is because it does not align with their beliefs, for others it is that the act of remaining fixed and stagnant is where they find comfort. The cultural humility approach shares the model of growth which depicts three overlapping circles, one larger than the next (Tervalon & Lewis, 2018). The largest circle is the panic zone, *Where disbelief lives, and fear stops all action*, the middle circle is the stretch zone, *Where excitement lives, action takes place, and fear disappears*, and the smallest circle is the comfort zone, *Where fear lives, action is limited or sporadic, and excitement wanes* (adapted from Masuria, 2012). Tervalon and Lewis (2018) quote Dean Seddon in sharing:

> The comfort zone is the place where apathy thrives, where motivation dies and the status quo remains. The panic zone is the place where there is too much pressure, the stakes are too high and living here will burn you out. In between those two areas is the stretch zone; this is the place where we find the right amount of challenge and the right level of pressure. This is where we should monitor our goals, and make sure we carry out an ambitious view on where to set our goals. Bodlovic and Jackson (2018) share how the concept of "stretching"

is used as a class assignment in their cultural considerations course in a Master's art therapy program. They also use Hays's "Becoming a culturally responsive therapist" (2001) to challenge students to explore why they may be apprehensive to adopt a culturally humble approach as they examine fear, ignorance, aversion to pain, desire, and egoism. In the self-reflective process, the art therapist must expose and educate themselves on their barriers to compassion to understand their biases and move to a place of advocacy for social equity.

## Social awareness in art therapy

Hogan and Pink (2010) used the term *social art therapy* to describe the social context in which individuals are viewed: this context includes *cultural and permeated power*. Social art therapy is concerned with universal discrimination and can challenge dominant discourses and provide a space in which to rehearse and explore strategies of resistance. Art therapy can cause viewers to question their discriminatory beliefs and practices that are encountered in everyday experiences. It can aid in reflecting and exploring the different sides of self while releasing the tensions between these alternate aspects of self. The self is also influenced by our lived experience within both social and power contexts. Part of one's self-identity within the field of art therapy is the identity of the art therapist.

Hays (2001) addressed the influence of the dominant culture as it underscored the importance of understanding social bias and power. Hays then addressed the relevance of staying humble while thinking critically, as well as noting obstacles to compassion and ways to overcome those obstacles.

Social change begins with cultural humility, which is fostered in the knowing of self. When practicing social change, art therapists must be mindful to understand their own values and not impose them on others, lest these values become another form of oppression. Levine and Levine (2011) cited Tervalon and Murray-Garcia's work, which addressed the need to acknowledge and rectify the power imbalance that exists in the dynamic of physician–patient communication through humility. Cultural humility helps develop and maintain mutually respectful relationships. In summary, Myers (1988) offered an overall solution to the problem:

> Our function is a cultural function: to redeem American culture from its segmented, sub-optimal Eurocentric conceptual system/ worldview… In knowing ourselves we must consider our origins. In our quest for truth, knowledge, identity, and oneness…let us consider the power and freedom of the subjective, and give honor to ourselves. (p.93)

Cultural humility began during a social political movement. When we are aware of social expressions in art we are creating a movement of our own within the artwork and therapeutic practice. Moving towards social justice charges the art therapist to welcome depictions and words reflecting the current political state unapologetically. Talwar *et al.* (2004) wrote:

> It becomes imperative for art therapy to revisit its cultural and social identities to become more inclusive. The incidents of racist attacks on individuals of visible racial-ethnic groups and the changing demographics of the United States are forcing art therapy to address issues of diversity. (p.44)

There is empowerment in allowing and encouraging clients to express the social and political influences on their lived experiences. These messages resound that this is our story and this is how we can help. Talwar *et al.* (2004) added, "in our view, lifting the veil implies that art therapists become change agents for transcending our legacy of ethnocentric monoculturalism" (p.47). The call for change agents must be met. This alludes to the notion that our jobs as art therapists go beyond the practice of our four walls; art therapists are called upon to assist in community building, following critical social and political incidents. Potash *et al.* (2015) stated:

> Such interventions require necessary knowledge and skills to repair relationships damaged by prejudice and systemic oppression; this is done by disseminating stories of marginalized persons, affirming diverse artistic traditions, and managing prejudice-based confrontations. (p.148)

This is to say that one's awareness of self, others, and social diversity does not have to be proclaimed on a soapbox accompanied by a specific, strong political stance. Rather, as Talwar *et al.* (2004), observed, "the arenas are the therapist's self and the clinical situation where diverse combinations of therapist and client encounter each other and have an authentic interaction within a matrix of deep awareness. This is sociopolitical action and social justice" (p.47).

Section 7.0 of the 2013 revised version of the AATA's Ethical Standards for practicing art therapists includes multicultural considerations that detail how art therapists must be aware of how the cultural background of clients impacts the therapeutic relationship. Art therapy practitioners are ethically required to be consciously aware of how their own biases affect their relationships with clients from different cultural backgrounds. According to the guidelines, practitioners are ethically responsible for gaining knowledge concerning how a client's cultural background influences their goals and values in therapy, and they must be adept at incorporating them into therapy sessions and treatment planning.

The field of art therapy has made significant inclusions for diverse art activities for cultural competency (Talwar, 2015). This includes activism in art therapy curriculum and art therapists using their skills and voices as a link to social change (Frostig, 2011; Potash, 2011). Although there is continuous research, specifically on how art therapists can develop cultural competence in the field of art therapy, significant change is necessary; the field of art therapy should continue its efforts regarding inclusion because art therapists constitute "a critical juncture in understanding the links between practice, culture, diversity, and identity as they relate to social justice" (Talwar, 2015, p.100).

Examining terms such as *social consciousness* and *freedom*, in classrooms, professional settings, and art therapy sessions" is necessary "if art therapy is to align itself with a social justice framework" and acknowledge "the reality that therapy is a social construct" (Gipson, 2015, p.143). Gipson elaborated on the relevance of cultural competence, but also the expansion of it to reach political awareness with safety:

As scholars have acknowledged, cultural competence has an important place in art therapy education. Yet we can invite a deeper commitment to issues of justice by examining power relations, insisting on inclusivity, and developing critical art therapy pedagogy that responds to all lives. (p.145)

Cultural humility addresses the power differential and encourages the individual and institution to examine privilege within social constructs. Talwar (2015) noted cultural competence has the tendency to become static when we label culture as a negative term that captures "isms." In this, she is not suggesting removing "diversity frameworks" but rather calling for "how can we build a collective vision, not one that only advocates for increasing awareness, but one that is transformative and grounded in equity and social justice?" (2015, p.100). When looking at diversity, equity, and inclusion within the organizations of the field of art therapy, including education systems, local chapters, and national organizations, it becomes imperative to make efforts to shift the power imbalance. There have been many who have offered suggestions through written works on ways to address this ongoing concern. A deliberate effort is needed to take the recommendations these resources offer to make shifts and changes, and to honor, recognize, and validate the voices both heard and unheard. Instead, we often over-utilize those who hold aspects of diversity in many different facets of the field. I often feel conflicted when asked to nominate or recommend someone of color, or other diversities, because those that I feel would be exceptional already hold positions in other areas of art therapy organizations. The acceptance of the recommendation or nomination may remove them from other areas where their voice and visual presence are needed, often in places not touched by the organization or field. We need to implement succession planning and mentorship that includes those from diverse backgrounds. Also, utilizing the suggestions that have been published over the past years, instead of muting or ignoring them, could begin to repair and restore relations within the field that may allow for a collective healing that acknowledges the social considerations that have impacted art therapy. Talwar (2015) further stated:

Our feelings arise directly from our social positions in culture and society. Art therapy from individualized, privatized models will do little to challenge oppressive conditions on a sociocultural level. To this end, when we locate art therapy within a social praxis, art making is no longer an intuitive process rooted in the unconscious; rather it becomes one that is collective, critical, conscious, and communal. (p.101)

## Recognizing biases, assumptions, and beliefs

One cannot turn a blind eye to the biases depicted in our art, behaviors, and practice. Whether covert or overt, they are there. Being aware of biases, beliefs, and assumptions gives understanding of one's worldview, an important element in being culturally humble. The myth in early diversity training spoke of being aware of biases, beliefs, and assumptions as aspects of the self that should be avoided, in a way similar to being colorblind (Acton, 2001). Ignoring one's histories, experiences, and memories prevents one from changing inappropriate biases, beliefs, and assumptions.

### Examining bias

There are three concepts that are important in the practice of art therapy, specifically, when addressing cultural humility. Those are biases, assumptions, and beliefs. We cannot deny these when enacted in the therapeutic space and much harm can come from not being aware of them. We will begin by exploring bias.

Why should we consider cultural variables when using art in the therapeutic process? Understanding the factors that may affect the therapeutic process can assist the art therapist in acknowledging his or her biases. Bias is defined as "a personal and sometimes unreasoned judgment" (Merriam-Webster, 2019d) or a "prejudice in favor of or against one thing, person, or group compared with another, usually in a way considered to be unfair" (Google Dictionary, n.d. a). Our biases are seen as developing from our intrapersonal communication related to our mental constructs, such as automatic thought processes manifested by our thinking styles

(Jun, 2010). Our biases, based on our feelings and attitudes related to characteristics such as "race, ethnicity, age, and appearance…are generally believed to develop over the course of a lifetime beginning at a very early age through exposure to direct and indirect messages" (Staats, 2014, p.16). Most often, when not reflective, we are unaware of our biases; this is now more commonly known as implicit bias, "an automatic and unconscious process, people who engage in this unthinking discrimination are not aware of the fact that they do it" (Wilkerson, 2013, p.134 as cited by Staats, 2014). We tend to modify our biases for social acceptability, although they still remain and affect our knowledge of cultural influences and how we view them.

Another consideration for potential bias, that appears to garner the least amount of attention, is power differential. Talwar (2010) reflected, "From my experience in the field of art therapy, I have found that issues of difference, power and authority mostly go unacknowledged"(p.11). Examining the media, including advertising, commercials, movies, and television, one can quickly perceive which ethnic and cultural group has the power. Talwar suggested that it is important for art therapists to investigate cultural constructs and examine the impact of visual media in determining how minority populations have been viewed. Power imbalance is one of the reasons that cultural humility offers a way of viewing cultures that have been marginalized.

### Assessing assumptions

Making assumptions is an everyday occurrence. This is where our biases become manifest or put into action. Assumption is defined as "1. A thing that is accepted as true or as certain to happen, without proof" and most importantly in regards to cultural humility "2. The action of taking on power or responsibility" (Google Dictionary, n.d. b). Many therapists sit in a place of power within the therapeutic space, impeding the collaborator the opportunity to be empowered. A culturally humble art therapist recognizes their power and makes efforts to create a balance within the space so that the collaborator can contribute to their own process. Assumptions are also defined as "the act of laying claim to or taking possession of something"

(Merriam-Webster, 2019b), much like appropriation, and can be just as dangerous. Assumptions cause us to disregard and not take into account someone's story. The cultural variables are ignored and what the therapist holds as "Truth" becomes true for the ones they are engaging with. Thereafter the story gets told through the therapist's cultural lens and worldview.

In *A Handbook for Developing Multicultural Awareness* author Paul B. Pedersen discusses cultural assumptions and a three-stage developmental framework which proceeds from awareness to knowledge to skill in defining necessary competencies through a needs assessment. Within its text, Pedersen gives several assumptions,

> First, culture is broadly and inclusively defined to include ethno-graphic, demographic, status and affiliation. Second, all counseling takes place in a multicultural context. Third, culture includes both the more obvious objective and the more hidden subjective perspectives of our identity. Fourth, both cultural similarities and cultural differences are equally important. Fifth, the most important insights of multicultural awareness can be learned but often cannot be directly taught. (2000, p.2)

Pedersen goes on to state that, "Competence begins with 'awareness' of your own culture in relationship with the other cultures around you, and an awareness of the culturally learned assumptions which control your life, with or without your permission" (p.4). Pedersen (2000) describes ten specific examples of cultural encapsulation by Western-trained counselors. One of these cultural assumptions is that "only linear, 'cause-effect' thinking is accepted as scientific and appropriate" (p.3).

## Exploring beliefs

Assumptions can be seen as synonymous with beliefs. In many ways, beliefs are linked to both assumptions and biases. They derive from our biases and they are things that we trust. Beliefs are defined as "1. A state or habit of mind in which trust or confidence is placed in some person or thing, 2. Something that is accepted, considered to be true, or held as an opinion" (Merriam-Webster, 2019c). Unlike an assumption, which can be challenging and often an act of taking for granted, a belief is a "3. Conviction of the truth, of some statement or the reality of some being or phenomenon especially when based on examination of evidence." (Merriam-Webster, 2019c). When held strongly and for long enough our assumptions become embedded beliefs. There are cases where we use our assumptions to validate our biases so that we have the evidence to conceptualize them as beliefs. Beliefs can also assist us through despair and offer us hope. In this way, many art therapists have belief in the healing of art. We need this belief to have confidence in the practice of art therapy, accept the method of art therapeutically, and through research examination hold it as an honest opinion. Lewis (1997) stated that art psychotherapists must be "sensitive about working with ethnically and culturally diverse individuals whose religious or spiritual beliefs are different than our own" (p.246). This has to be considered while also understanding that transcendence can move individuals beyond these beliefs.

## Benefits and challenges

One of the most challenging practices of cultural humility is implementing the principles within institutions that struggle with barriers to compassion. There are both struggles and benefits to using a culturally humble approach in art therapy when faced with institutionalized oppression and discrimination and yet the principles call for one to advocate and maintain institutional accountability. This is necessary for the principles to be effective and change to occur within systems that are designed to amplify the power and privilege of some and contain the marginalization and dehumanization of others. When placed in a position where, within a system, institution, and/or facility, the art therapist (clinician) is the only one making the efforts to incorporate cultural humility, the challenge becomes that of feeling burned out due to having to be the constant spokesperson for equity, diversity, and inclusion. It is at these moments that an ally is needed. Actively taking the stance to come forth and support those who are bringing social change into a space takes courage and can be a benefit and help.

There are many forms of social justice advocacy. When moving in cultural humility, one guides and leads by example in conjunction with educating. This may not always be received well, as those who are unfamiliar with the practice may see it as a threat to their way of being. Part of being culturally humble is being aware of villainizing those who may not be using the principles, while having awareness of self in the space and how one might be impacting or impeding the principles from being received. When approaching the space with humility, what can be perceived as a challenge can be moved to modeling and educating. One model that offers a culturally humble approach is the "Guidelines for interaction—Dr. King's principles" (Potash & Gymiah-Boadi, 2018). The model asks the art therapist to be active in analyzing one's self, developing a center of goodness, defeating the system, cutting off the chain of hate, and refraining from dehumanizing (Potash & Gymiah-Boadi, 2018). At times when advocating for equity our frustrations can overwhelm us because of the severe nature of the pain that is felt when oppressed or persecuted. It is at these moments that being culturally humble is most challenging. In non-violent movements such as Dr. King's, many took to sitting in as an action. This activism echoes calling people *in* versus calling them *out*, which can often lead to defensiveness, retaliation, and attack (Potash, 2018). Cultural humility can help civility be found when there is a potential for it to be lost. It does not mean ignoring the social dynamics and the harmful destruction that it can elicit. As shared by Potash (2018) there is room for "both being 'at the table' and 'in the streets'" (p.203). Being culturally humble reminds us to be aware and act accordingly so as to cause movement and change.

In art therapy, understanding social dynamics and being mindful of being colorblind becomes an underlining aspect of remaining culturally humble. Social dynamics, often displayed through power imbalance, can be seen in the therapeutic relationship, the art, and the art process, and in the art therapist's assessment of the client. Once addressing the power dynamics in the therapeutic space, the art therapist must then align with the community, recognizing space metaphorically, but literally as well. Institutions like schools, hospitals, and treatment centers can provoke and perpetuate social dynamics. Because of the inequality that can exist in these systems, when the art therapist begins equalizing the engagement with the client, those spaces can assist in bolstering self-awareness within the art therapist and move the art therapist and those systems toward social change. The awareness then comes recognizing the cultural considerations within a community. Having social advocacy is responding to those considerations to enact social change.

Responding to cultural considerations can begin with recognizing that in many societies oppression and marginalization come from the perception or reality that there is a lack of resources, causing a struggle over resources. Resources take many forms: human beings, manual labor or manpower, materials, and access to information or knowledge. The lack of or the ampleness of resources determines where we live, what we can afford, and how we perceive the world (moral judgment) (Pitesa & Thau, 2014). It can affect our mood, self-esteem, sense of vulnerability, and sense of status and power, creating imbalance and barriers. Being disenfranchised can also result in alternatives, action, and advocacy, leading us to the past and current movements which many art therapists have and continue to engage in (Talwar, 2019). To directly respond to cultural considerations, an art therapist can offer resources, educate clients about community resources, show clients how to access resources, and bring resources into the institution.

One of the best ways to respond through advocacy is by being part of the community. Often, art therapists arrive to offer their services then leave to return to a community less impacted by the lack of resources. By engaging in events and visiting the community (neighborhood) an art therapist transitions from their comfort zone to their stretch zone. Stretching (Bodlovic & Jackson, 2018) includes talking with others about injustices and discoveries once stretched. Remaining open to hearing all voices, even those you are at odds with, is the culturally humble way of engaging in dialogue. When approaching interaction from this open space, it can shift or change a bias, assumption, or belief, if we are present to hear what the different ways of thinking and being are in the space, and why those different approaches to the world may have developed. If this approach is not being received, try another method or find another way into the space; this may be another person, venue, or offering. Assuming that those who oppose our beliefs are radical or indignant is informed by our thinking styles, which often impact our interactions with others, based on our developed explicit or implicit biases (Jun, 2010). While being with the client and the community is essential, changing the system from within by being part of the system can also disseminate equity and change. Allowing others to witness a culturally humble approach and spreading a new ideology amongst those who may share a homogeneous way of thinking and being can also shift stagnated systems, institutions, and organizations.

It is imperative for an art therapist to know when and how taking a stance may lead to harm. Physical safety must be considered before all else. Many different ways of approaching advocacy through art have been documented and observed. In history, all forms of art have been used, including sculptures, murals, monuments, slogans, graphic posters, comics, symbols, colors, propaganda, songs, chants, writings, poetry, and dance. More recently, we have seen digital advocacy such as hashtags and memes. Taking to the streets and protesting is not the only way, although visible and necessary at times. Standing with those who have less privilege and power may simply mean creating a space for their voices to be heard. Many communities have existing power; art therapists must not assume that it does not exist. Many communities have been healing themselves and have methods of healing already in place. Highlighting this inner strength through art advocacy and art therapy empowers the community and opposes further oppression and marginalization.

Growing towards multicultural attunement should be a lifelong endeavor. Competence should not be an end goal, but a way of life. When I think about the factors I have integrated into my framework of understanding, I would highlight the concept of cultural humility. While striving to be more attuned, the factor that I have the most challenge with is "Awareness of own values, beliefs, attitudes, and biases regarding self...regarding others" (George, Greene, & Blackwell, 2005, p.132). The challenge has derived from that fact that my awareness of others and myself continues to change as I grow and mature, travel, gain more experience in my career, learn about myself, and discover new cultures and new ways of being.

How I perceive myself continues to evolve. This causes a change in the interactions I have with my clients, others around me and the communities I serve. What I have valued has become solidified, while also changing to meet the needs of the environments that I am in. There is a flexibility and openness in my beliefs, attitudes, and biases beginning to arise through my extending and increasing knowledge. Hays (2001) links critical thinking and humility as one of the ways to becoming an effective therapist. He quotes Brookfield in stating, "critical thinking skills are essential to humility because they involve the abilities to identify and challenge assumptions (one's own as well as those of others), examine contextual influences (on one's own thinking too), and imagine and explore alternatives (p.25). Using both critical thinking and humility are ways I hope to address overcoming my challenges related to self-awareness, awareness of others, and communities. Allowing my self to continue to strengthen my knowledge while understanding that others and communities are experts on their own culture, and I have just as much to learn from them.

## REFLECTIVE PERSPECTIVE

**Meanings by Claudia Itzel Marquez,
unpublished thesis, 2018**

**Illumination:** The moment of illumination occurred while I created art in the studio before class. It was in that moment that I realized that this research was not about what it means to work with marginalized youth; rather, this research was about exploring personal and collective experiences that we (I and the youth I worked with) share and how these collective experiences define the therapeutic space our relationship exists in. Journaling and creating art as a means of self-reflection helped define the role that I, and everything I embody, play in the context of the therapeutic relationships between myself and the students I worked with. It was a process of bridging the therapeutic space with experiences that we both share and, at the same time, honoring that we stand on different parts of that bridge.

The purpose of this research was to investigate what it means to work with marginalized communities, specifically with high school students of Mesoamerican descent. The heuristic research methodology set at the forefront my personal experience. Through the process of critical self-reflection, I arrived at my own self-discoveries and understanding of what it means to me, a Xicana art therapist trainee, to provide mental health services to students of a background similar to my own. Based on the analysis of the data, the following concepts were prevalent in the journal entries and artwork: identity, family, community, validation, grounding, and healing. The relational reflections provide context for the concepts that emerged. In addition, the relational reflections served as containers in which I applied an intersectional framework to identify the multiple characteristics of identity, family, and community as they relate to the imbalance of power and systems of oppression (Kuri, 2017; Talwar, 2010).

Identity refers to my intersecting identities, which, as I mentioned before, are the foundations of my frame of reference. My family history and dynamics, too, were prevalent themes in my reflections because the families I worked with were of similar backgrounds to my own. The basis of relatedness is in the cultural, societal, economic, institutional, and historical contexts that we exist in as a community.

The exploration of these concepts in my reflective process allowed for examination of my values, biases, assumptions, and beliefs. Identity, family, and community inform my worldviews and my views impact the way in which I understand myself in relation to others, in this case, the students I worked with. Self-awareness of my intersecting identities, family history and dynamics, and my role both as a member of the community and MFT art therapy trainee, informed greatly my understanding of the space we exist in relation and the space between us that differentiates our similar experiences ("we" in this case refers to the students, family, and myself, who are all part of the same community). This process consisted of examining my biases and assumptions about working in the community I was raised in (Calisch, 2003; Kapitan, 2015; Talwar *et al.*, 2004).

Validation, grounding, and healing were essential to integrating myself back into my community as a clinician in training. Validation of students' subjugated narratives and of my own were significant in creating affirming and supportive therapeutic relationships. Validation of my own views, feelings, experiences, and countertransference in the therapeutic space led to increased awareness of how they all inform my therapeutic approach. I realized that my responsibility to my community as a self-identified woman of color shaped my values and influenced my understanding of my MFT art therapist identity.

Grounding experiences were necessary in maintaining clarity and humility. I often found myself feeling stuck because of tension between Eurocentric theoretical frameworks and my own approach to conceptualizing clinical cases, my responsibility as a trainee working for a DMH-contracted agency and my responsibility to my community, and from interrelatedness between myself and the students, I worked with. For each point of tension, I relied on self-reflection and the application of an intersectional framework to identify areas of relatedness and differentiation (Kuri, 2017; Talwar, 2010).

Active engagement in my own healing was also necessary in understanding further my relation to self and others. Particularly, in making meaning of my experiences and interrelatedness with the students I worked with. The students I worked with and I share a collective consciousness. Through the process of simultaneously supporting them in their own growth and engaging in my reflective process, I increased my insight and understanding of my adverse childhood experiences. Ceremony is a place where I reflect and connect with others, the elements, and my senses in order to have transformative healing experiences. In my efforts to bridge overlapping identities and experiences, I found myself having more questions than answers. I thought deeply about what healing means to me, which led to exploring what a healing experience is and finally to asking myself how I could engage with the students I worked with to co-create healing experiences for both of us. I intentionally say both of us because we exist together in relation to one another and the therapeutic relationship also has an impact on me, the therapist. There is a fine line of course because it is the therapists' responsibility to find an appropriate space to process their experiences, a space to self-reflect. This is significant to my findings because although the literature explains what, it is up to the individual to define how and where.

In brief, what these concepts reveal is critical self-reflection of one's biases, values, and beliefs as they relate to one's own privilege and oppression. The literature in the field of art therapy regarding work with marginalized communities emphasizes the importance of self-reflexivity and self-awareness of systems of power and oppression (Gipson, 2015; Golub, 2005; Hocoy, 2005; Kapitan, 2015; Kuri, 2017; Talwar, 2010). The journal entries and the art convey various levels of self-reflection that acknowledge intersecting identities and relations. The research process affirms the importance of self-reflection. Although the art therapy literature addresses other areas of attention (i.e., education, training, research, and theoretical models), this research speaks specifically to my experience as an MFT art therapy trainee working in my hometown and the importance of self-reflection in defining my identity by examining intersecting identities and subjugated narratives (Gipson, 2015).

## RESPONSE ART

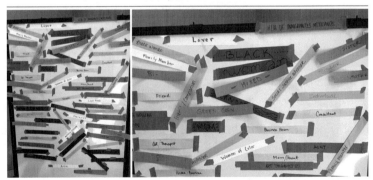

*Figure 5.2 Collaborative art from Social Commons, 2018*

## REFLECTIVE EXERCISE E: **ADDRESSING ASSUMPTIONS, BIASES, AND BELIEFS**

■ **Goal:** To explore intrapersonal communication that can lead to biases, assumptions, and beliefs.

"Intrapersonal communication is a mirror image of one's cultural values, beliefs, and biases... Endless internal repetition of a message lead to an illusion that the message is based on facts rather than based on the repeated self-talk (intrapersonal communication)" (Jun, 2010, p.21). Jun suggests that our biases are developed through our intrapersonal communication, which reflects our thought patterns (p.26). These thinking styles are described as (a) Holistic: Individuals with this thinking style are able to give equal weight to their opinions as well as those of others; (b) Linear: It is *projecting* and generalizing on the basis of the past...assuming that things, and people stay regardless of sociocultural contextual changes, time changes, and developmental stages; (c) Hierarchical: When individuals out others or themselves into a superior or inferior position; (d) Dichotomous: Conceptualizing within an "either/or" mindset, which leads to only two extremes (pp.27–33).

Where does it come from?

■ **Materials:** Structured materials: paper, markers, pencils, crayons, colored paper, scissors, and glue.

■ **Prompt 1:** Assessing thought process and intra-communication.

1. List ten frequently used thoughts, feelings and statements you repeat to yourself.

   Try not to edit or filter your statements. Write down what first comes to mind as quickly and spontaneously as possible.

   What are your patterns?

2. Determine what thinking styles your statements fall under.

   Write an H, L, Hi or D next to each statement.

How does it affect practice?

3. Examine what percentage was the largest thinking style used? Create an image symbolizing your most used thinking style.

■ **Q&A:** Do you recall the first time you were exposed to this thinking style? If possible, dialogue with someone about your discoveries. If in class, have students find a partner.

■ **Resolve:** Close your eyes (at your comfort) while breathing in and out slowly and evenly. Reflect on your relationship with your thinking style. Write down your relationship with intra-communication (changes, challenges, encouragement).

■ **Debiasing:** Write down a holistic statement summarizing your relationship with your thinking pattern (i.e., "I am realizing that I have a tendency to use linear thinking and I will work on ways to expand my patterns").

■ **Goal:** To explore how we can act on our biases through assumptions. Often we act or make decisions based on our assumptions. Throughout the day, make note of the assumptions you make about places, people and things.

■ **Materials:** Paper, markers, pencils, crayons, colored paper, tissue paper, scissors and glue, collage images and model magic, yarn, and other decorative items.

■ **Prompt 2:** Examining assumptions: Self-reflection.

1. Sit with yourself and write down assumptions you observed that you made throughout the day and those you may be making at the current moment. Think about assumptions you make based on age, religion, ethnicity, region, ability, etc.

2. If you are able, share with someone what you may have discovered from doing this exercise. If in class, form small groups.

3. Create a self-reflective piece on how it felt to honestly examine your assumptions. Explore the feelings associated with self.

■ **Resolve:** Create a positive affirmation of self and share with someone or group (i.e., use "I" statement).

■ **Goal:** To examine how we can hold our assumptions as truths. There are many types of beliefs that an individual may have. Some are clearly defined and stand alone and some are intertwined. Some we vocalize or share through image and word and others we hold without consciously or unconsciously externalizing them. Staats (2014) shares that our implicit biases "do not necessarily align with our declared beliefs or even reflect stances we would explicitly endorse" (p.17).

■ **Materials:** Paper, markers, pencils, crayons, colored paper, scissors and glue, collage images, and model magic, yarn and other decorative items, paint, watercolor, tissue paper, and fabric.

■ **Prompt 3:** Patterns of belief: religion, spirituality, and cultural beliefs.

1. Write down all of your beliefs.

■ **Q&A:** What experiences changed or solidified your beliefs? Which beliefs are steadfast and have not changed?

2. Dialogue with someone about your beliefs.

If in class, have students' dialogue in small groups.

If with someone or in class, after dialogue, create art together in silence. Then discuss.

Share the process of incorporating beliefs and the importance of beliefs in practice.

■ **Resolve:** Create an art piece celebrating beliefs that have expanded your humility and understanding of others and self.

# CHAPTER 6

# Introspection and Self-Care

*Mandala: Circular Pattern of Humility, Cycles, Coming Full Circle*

*Figure 6.1 Collective Study Collaborator Art 007*

## Importance of self-reflection in cultural humility

"Perhaps the most central issue concerns the potential for art therapy to perpetuate Western cultural imperialism" (Hocoy, 2002, p.141). It is this historical and current factor that ensures culturally diverse training, education, and awareness are needed. Hocoy continues by conveying that, due to the reflected and reinforced Western therapeutic traditions, "Art therapy has an opportunity to respond differently through self-critique and conscientious attempts to be a progressive and culturally sensitive enterprise" (p.144). In sharing the cultural humility principles, Hocoy offers guidelines for art therapists to become critically self-aware and mindful of biases, assumptions, and beliefs about others in a cultural context in order to move away from art therapy's Euro-American foundations:

> First, the art therapist would benefit from engaging in rigorous and honest self-examination as to his or her cultural competency. This involves an awareness of one's own cultural lens, as well as an awareness of the assumptions and values on which theory and technique in art therapy are based. It also involves awareness of any personal uneasiness concerning appearance, smell, nonverbal behaviors, physical proximity, worldviews, accents, and limited English of people from other cultures. Work with one's personal issues may be necessary with regard to addressing conscious and unconscious attitudes and biases towards diversity and difference. (2002, p.144)

Discussions of diversity, equity and inclusion have continued in art therapy, particularly in relation to self-awareness. Art therapists such as Kapitan (2015) speak about shifting the ethnocentric lens with the focus on first broadening "the lens...to reflectively examine and discard inaccurate assumptions and engage in critical reflection" (p.106). ter Maat (2011) shared:

> Cultural awareness refers to the therapist's sensitivity to his or her own assumptions about human nature and behavior; values, beliefs, and attitudes toward one's own culture; and the cultural experiences that shaped one's personality (Sue & Sue, 2008). Cultural self-awareness begins with self-questioning... Searching for answers to

these questions is a necessary first step in the internal and lifelong process of acquiring cultural competence. (p.5)

The first important aspect of self-reflection is to engage in it creatively (Jackson, 2016). Creative self-reflection can alleviate possible suffering for those we serve if an art therapist engages in it through continuous practice. Moon (2015) shares, "The commitment to live creatively in accordance to what they teach is one of the qualities that makes art therapists therapeutic persons" (p.98). If not participating in art as a continuous practice, the art therapist can be removed from the significance of self-reflection with the tools of the profession. Without being closely engaged in art reflection, an art therapist may begin to minimize or become detached from the effects of the art-making process: "Without a solid sense of self, art therapist can unintentionally impede the self-exploration and self-expression of their client" (Moon, 2015, p.98). I had not realized how distant I had become from the creative process until I began re-engaging in art through my PhD program. I had been doing art as part of preparation for my clients and assisted my clients with their creative journey. I had not participated in art as a tool for reflection or self-care as I once did. Although I was present for my clients a deeper empathy and compassion was missing as I began to get burned out without knowing why. It becomes easy to say we don't have the time or there are too many other things to do. Once in a routine of not using art for myself, it became easier to make justifications about why I was not using it. It was not until much later I realized that I had diverted my creative energy toward dance instead of art. Dance had been a way for me to heal from the inside and out. It had become spiritual and a way for me to self-reflect creatively using my body as my art tool. I now know I needed that kinesthetic engagement to help release the vicarious trauma I was holding. It lifted the veil of discontent and offered me a renewed energy. Going to dance class every Friday evening and participating in the dance community was both my self-reflection and self-care. Participating in my doctoral program caused me to postpone my regular engagement in dance and my dance community. And it also brought me back to the creative arts that I had disengaged from. When I re-engaged with it, I once again connected to healing through visual art, which enhanced my level of creativity and stimulated my inquisitiveness for more knowledge, setting a precedent for practicing cultural humility.

Through continuous art practice, an art therapist can develop stronger empathy and congruence. A key component of cultural humility is self-reflection and a lifelong inquiry into understanding those we serve and with whom we work. Using art reflection can assist the art therapist in working through countertransference that may block the flow of trust between client and art therapist. It can also help the art therapist to have a clearer understanding of themselves in order to communicate more effectively with diverse populations. Ongoing self-reflection through practice can enhance an art therapist's ability to walk a mile in someone else's shoes. It helps an art therapist to adhere to ethical standards: good communication, such as trust, accountability, mutual respect, and fair care. Also, if the public is aware that art therapists are dedicated to the practice of art therapy themselves through the continuous practice of art, it can promote positive ethical practices for the profession. Supporting ethics in art therapy, Moon (2015) states, "in order to have creditability in advocating for self-discovery and self-expression in client's lives, it is important for art therapists to authentically engage in artistic discovery and expression in their own lives" (p.98). This may cause a more integrated approach to art therapy that involves the collaboration of practice; not the practice of an etic but an emic approach.

Self-reflection in cultural humility is not only facilitated to foster awareness. It is a critical process that necessitates both expressing and involving oneself in an analysis of merits and faults. Having critical introspection requires an art therapist to not only become aware of self, it also challenges the art therapist to analyze and take action towards change and reflection. Moon (2015) expresses that, "sometimes creative self-exploration leads to change" (p.95). A crucial self-reflective process promotes transparency and a willingness to engage honestly with others. This builds strength-based intuition that transforms into trust building with clients and others. When art therapists can trust themselves because they have reflected on challenging aspects such as blind spots, weaknesses, and inferiorities, they can convene in the therapeutic space with confidence and meaning. Along with bringing into the therapeutic space the competencies we are taught, an art therapist also brings their personhood (Moon, 2015). Moon further elaborates that the humanity of our identity encompasses our "life story, desires, longings, strengths, weakness, successes, frustrations, values, and fears" (p.98). Accountability can develop from having awareness of our difficult attributes such as weakness; it can also convey humility when it is vocalized to others. Speaking on our weakness offers us an opportunity to strengthen our character and display humanness.

## Circular process of cultural humility

By observing and interacting with many perspectives and self-reflecting concurrently, I delved into the depths of interrelation in self-awareness, extracting a circular process, truth, balance, and self-care. When using the critical self-reflective process of cultural humility, it is observed that each engagement, experience, and self-reflective work takes place in a non-linear process. Each has its own beginning and end without directly reflecting or responding to the previous reflection as in a linear manner. In cultural humility, our engagements, activities, and interactions with others build on previous experiences that each person has lived through, giving them a context in which to view their current lived experience. To reflect humbly means having thoughts of the future, and then again to ponder on current reflections, conveying a story that is without a clear beginning, middle, and end. Like the Sankofa bird (pictured in Figure 6.2), appearing to move forward, holding the future, while looking back and honoring our individual past and shared experiences as art therapists and other professionals. Concurrently, every encounter experienced brings one back and then forward again with an adjusted view. From each experience, we move forward with revitalized concepts and beliefs, as well as doubt and insecurity. With some movements, our circle will expand, and with others the circle will retract itself, intensifying. In this way, knowledge is either increased or validated, but not stagnant. This is an example of ways of knowing that are other than linear in cultural humility.

*Figure 6.2 Collective Study Collaborator Art 017*

Cox's tripartite model, shown in the article "A redefinition of multicultural counseling" (Speight *et al.*, 1991), illustrates the optimal redefinition of multiculturalism. This collaboration of circular dimensions was designed by Cox in 1982 to depict a worldview in which cultural specificity, individual uniqueness, and human universality interact to influence individuals. To get a full understanding of an individual one must explore all three aspects. To further elaborate, multiculturalism should not concentrate on one of these circles but on where all three overlap. It is where these three circles overlap that they begin to "capture the richness of individuals" (Speight *et al.*, 1991, p.32). It is this holistic view of an individual that is the foundation of optimal theory. The influences on an individual's worldview lead to the concept of thinking about culture in a circular context and could be incorporated into art therapy through the depiction of the mandala linking cultural humility, art therapy, and the optimal theory. The link is a circular connection that brings awareness to all three aspects. Bringing a non-Eurocentric view to art therapy through optimal therapy can enhance the education of cultural humility in the field. This cultural enrichment, that has been expressed as a need in art therapy, can be facilitated through the education of self-awareness in art therapists by simultaneously reflecting through all three concepts.

The optimization process is a circular process in which individualistic environmental influences emphasize a separate sense of self and therefore a suboptimal worldview. For people of color, this experience of self can be reinforced through environmental pressures (e.g., racism) so that the individual comes to experience the self as increasingly separate and alienated; the response to these negative experiences is anger and anxiety. When there are opportunities to grow in self-knowledge, which is represented as the "true nature of the self" in optimal therapy, the transformation of the self occurs (Myers, 1988). In art therapy collaboration, either through therapeutic practice or research study, the collective experience of sharing the creative process, particularly with those with similar cultural identities, can encourage a more multidimensional and infinite sense of self. In this process, one grows in awareness of a spiritual dimension to self, an increasing awareness of the divine, which is marked by a sense of peace. This leads to an optimal worldview (Myers, 1988). In the process one may share reflections of anger/anxiety separation and negative experiences, and sharing the creative process can give the artists an opportunity to grow in collective self-awareness. The circular process of mandalas in art therapy connects with the circular implications of optimal theory. *Creating Mandalas* describes the life process as a growth cycle where "The archetype of the Self governs the natural cycle of individuation" (Fincher, 1991, p.148). Similar to cultural humility, the practice spirals upwards then back down again. The engagement into one principle often layers on top of the next until you begin the cycle over again. Competence is never truly gained, as each life experience activates a new level of growth and understanding. This process of cultural humility again relates to the great round, which cycles to reveal another layer of self towards one's whole being. Fincher (2009) stated:

> Unlike many developmental theories that posit a linear progression from simpler, less mature states to more complex mature states, the concept of the Great Round is grounded in ancient ideas of life as a spiraling journey toward greater wisdom and wholeness. In this way of looking at life, all your experiences are viewed as meaningfully placed on a cycle that revolves around the Self as you more and more fulfill your potential wholeness. (p.26)

Described in this circular process, each new lived experience offers a unique engagement into becoming culturally humble. Sometimes it feels familiar, extending a place for transformation. At times it is a newly gained space, moving self into transcendence. Fincher continues:

> The mandala serves conservation purpose-namely, to restore a previously existing order. But it also serves the creative purpose of giving expression and form to something that does not yet exist, something new and unique... The purpose is that of the ascending spiral, which grows upward while simultaneously returning again and again to the same point. (p.126)

When critically self-reflecting and viewing culture through a non-linear, non-Western lens an art therapist can gain a sense of cultural humility regardless of their ethnic background. Lavery (1994) stated that being able to illustrate one's own views could be beneficial: "Art therapists can use this method to gain insight into themselves and to enhance their ability to relate to their clients" (p.14). Further, "Making art gives me a greater awareness of myself and also keeps my creativity active" (p.14). Using art to explore cultural humility can give a clinician a greater awareness. Self-knowledge, expression through mandalas, the teaching of optimal therapy, and the understanding of culture can bring about a non-Eurocentric, non-linear awareness of cultural humility in art therapy and the self-reflective process. The over-layering aspects of self-awareness, culture, optimization, and creation can offer us insight into one's truth.

## Exploring the truth in cultural humility

The search for "Truth" can be subjective and is often Westernized to mean self-actualization (Maslow, 1943). Foucault viewed the self, which was initially proposed by Freud and accepted into Western culture as truth, to be "illusory" (Martin & Barresi, 2008, p.261). Foucault hoped to elevate the notion of culture as a construct that is tied to individuals and the power dynamics necessary to foster individual freedom. In this endeavor, he wanted to reintroduce the "practice of care of self," whereby what was presumed to be the "'truth' about the self, and knowledge in general, depended on active concern for and care of the self" (Martin & Barresi, 2008, p.261). This practice does not "include finding a deep, inner truth but, rather governing 'one's own life in order to give it the most beautiful form possible'" (p.261). Some cultures have less concern about discovering a deep inner truth and a greater concern about creating a life worth living through reflecting on life's experiences and the experience of the community. For some, searching for the meaning of self is reserved for the privileged and collegiate. Foucault stated that the ongoing search for meaning is not liberating but instead enslaving (Martin & Barresi, 2008). He understood that searching for one's true self was problematic because the true self was not something tangible that could be obtained like an object, but rather something one had to create or construct (Martin & Barresi, 2008). hooks (1993) expressed from a Black woman's perspective the difficulty in depicting her truth and how this can lead to stress. She spoke about the Black woman's need to wear a mask to hide her truth in order to become accepted by society. She stated, "It is not easy for a black female to be dedicated to the truth. And yet the willingness, to be honest, is essential for our well-being" (p.27). This hiding may be done in other cultural groups who fear being recognized by the dominant culture who often berate what they don't understand. This level of concern for one's safety becomes so ingrained that it is difficult to let down one's guard. Even in the presence of an art therapist, who pushes clients to share and show more of their "true" self, according to psychological theory, some cultures may feel unsafe to explore.

In cultural humility, self-critique is not done for fulfillment of a higher meaning, as in Western humanistic theory and psychologists such as Carl Roger's "real self" or "ideal self"; instead it is an intentional exploration to acknowledge the truth of being at that present moment in time (İsmail & Tekke, 2015). Because this truth can be subjective and change, a culturally humble critique must be done on an ongoing basis, at times cycling or spiraling back through. The drive for the authentic self can go against some cultures. And it is through the awareness of one's own beliefs that an art therapist needs to be careful in creating directives that guide clients in that way. Particularly when coming from a more collectivist culture, this approach may not fit all. It is a Western concept that has been imbedded in idealism of the white male perspective in the United States, that has been adapted by some and acknowledged by others. Unlike Western psychology, a field Hogan (2016) describes as reflecting "the individualistic masculine capitalism of mid-twentieth-century North America" (p.68), cultural humility is not a linear growth pattern where the ultimate goal is to reach self-actualizing. Instead it is holistic and offers an integrated approach that can apply to many cultures, ideals, and concepts, including outside the dominant culture.

## Optimal theory and self-knowledge

Optimal therapy, introduced by Myers (1988), provides an integrated approach to training practitioners to work with a variety of populations. Optimal theory's psychotherapeutic approach integrates psychodynamic, cognitive-behavioral, and humanistic aspects (Speight et al., 1991). The optimization process supports collaborative ways of knowing emphasized in both training and practice and moves from a suboptimal view of the world that fosters societal "isms," to an optimal view of the world that values diversity. Myers's (1988) non-Western/non-Eurocentric theory offers a holistic, self-knowledge aspect to diversity that could be beneficial to art therapy education and practice.

Further, optimal psychology offers an Afrocentric approach to truth and knowledge that can be integrated with art therapy. Myers

(1988) proposed that self-knowledge is the basis of all knowledge, and that "good science" not only acknowledges subjectivity but also explores its exact nature in detail in order to reveal "true" knowledge. The Afrocentric way of knowing reflects ancient African writings: "Ancient Africans built their science on the realization of the value of the subjective. This is evident in the epistemology assumption that self-knowledge is the basis of all knowledge, and that one knows through symbolic imagery and rhythm" (Myers, 1988, p.91). Unlike cultural competence, cultural humility is interconnected with truth, gives power to each voice, is personal, authentic, organic, mutually developed, and skill based. It includes dialogue, reflection, and ongoing, fluid, engagement. It allows all those involved to be the learner or student. It is teachable, encompasses partnership, shared decision-making, and is flexible and dynamic (Tervalon, 2015). The critical self-reflection and lifelong learning in cultural humility ask the practitioner to know your own identity and what you are bringing into the interaction and in what ways are you bringing your identity, power, and privilege to work (Tervalon & Lewis, 2018). In the self-critique clinicians are courageously asking themselves: What do I think about this cultural group(s)? How do I know this to be true? What are my biases? What are they based on? What are the consequences in my relationship with this person, this community, if I act on these biases? What can I learn here? And how? What are my responsibilities? (Tervalon & Lewis, 2018).

In art therapy, an art therapist must allow their client to depict their own truth within the art. What may be difficult for clients to convey in other modalities can come through with conviction in this process. The art allows the client to not only recreate and design their own truth; if done collectively or in the witness of others, including the art therapist, their art can acknowledge aspects of themselves and give them permission to convey their own truth as well. The truth depicted through the lived experience of the client can appear to offer what resonates as wisdom. Empowering the client by acknowledging their wisdom, as a contribution to their therapeutic journey, and offering guidance while utilizing their strengths is one of the delicate balances of cultural humility.

## The balance of cultural humility

The circular process of cultural humility allows for the practitioner to hold different perspectives as truth, deriving a balanced "both/ and" worldview. Cycling through and repeatedly reflecting on the material is a method of checks and balances that supports a heuristic approach; in this technique, the researcher continuously reflects, looking at the work from different perspectives while challenging and validating assumptions. This process can also be done to offer a balanced perspective in self-critique within cultural humility. The balance of cultural humility facilitates holding, learning, love, growth, acceptance, courage, and peace while also releasing, feeling frustration, disregard, and despair. These concepts relate strongly to the balance of cultural humility and what it means to be humble when addressing diversity within our lives and with those we serve.

Cultural humility encompasses being vigilant of individual goals, awareness, worldview, and collective influences (values, beliefs, and assumptions) with humility. Wholeness includes both one's individual and collective selves. Becoming culturally humble, with humility, love, and courage, within one's whole self, occurs in continuous, sustained self-reflection (art, journal, intrapersonal dialogue) and persistent cultural proficiency (skill, knowledge, practice). This is all done in balance (interrelatedness). It includes allowing those with whom one collaborates to be seen and heard while acknowledging their whole presence. Being culturally humble must be a transformative learning process: "learning to integrate intellectual understanding (knowledge) with emotional understanding (affect)" (Jun, 2010, p.9). As an art therapist engages in both individual and collective worldviews through art (affect), while also engaging in continued cultural diversity training (knowledge), this can allow for the participation in the knowledge and the affect of transformative learning.

Cultural humility is a delicate balance in art therapy because of the need to balance the self in the art in conjunction with the collective. We may be culturally connected to others as a group and universally belong to the individualist society of the United States of America, which, many have expressed, develops into a conflict associated with what appears to be collectivist ways of knowing.

Allowing for a culturally humble stance may mean balancing collective knowing with specific family values, which would be individualized based on region, age, parentage, and socioeconomic status. Being a part of US society, societal reinforcements coming from a Western individualistic worldview may impact our efforts to become culturally humble and effectively self-reflect.

Often the perception of self is defined through family, ethnicity, tribe, community, and nationality of that society. When individuals from that society choose to speak out for their individual rights or self-concept they are often labeled as rebellious, disobedient, and/or disrespectful, which in turn can be perceived as going against other members of the group (David, 2008). Having a culturally humble stance may mean holding our self-concept while remaining supportive of the dominant group, even if they differ in what they represent. Seamlessly and eloquently, within my collective research study, many of the collaborators' journal entries referred to being a Black woman, while also expressing their individual thoughts and reflections (Jackson, 2016). David (2008) also expressed the shared values of the collectivist as "harmony, cooperation, respect, loyalty, modesty and satisfying the needs of others" (p.2). This statement conveys the link to cultural humility and how most of the women from the study inherently expressed these values in their art depictions and words. In collectivist societies, women often feel that they represent their collective as well as themselves, and, because of this sense of identity, their thinking and behavior are directed more toward collectivist values (David, 2008).

There is difficulty in determining how to move beyond the individual client to the thoughts and expressions of the collective. Being open, one's worldview as an art therapist, which includes the individual, while moving beyond the social constructs and foundations of one's community and society, can be challenging. Often, in my practice to become culturally humble, I work at being aware and maintaining the balance of my individual biases, beliefs, and goals with my collective assumptions, values, and connections. By constantly using intuition, I am able to navigate new experiences and cultural immersions. As in a continuing cycle, I have gone through this balance during many experiences in my life. It is important to balance the knowledge that one fosters and innately holds with the understanding that that knowledge does not make one an expert of another's lived experience. One's privilege as an art therapist is the education one has acquired. It is important to not hold this privilege over one's clients and so have that privilege become another form of oppression. This idea is further elaborated by Jun (2010), who stated, "Balancing the art component with the knowledge (scientific) component throughout the therapeutic process is crucial for effective treatment" (p.409). Jun noted that the art component, which consists of rapport, supportiveness, empathy, active listening, trust, and acceptance, couldn't be taught. The importance of the heart and mind were empathized in the metaphors of heart and mind; the heart meaning creative aspects, and the mind, the more scientific way of knowing through words. If using a culturally humble approach, both art and mind are needed to offer a holistic balance. Again, this balance is supported by Jun (2010):

> The knowledge component interacts with the art component dynamically. The practitioner is present with both heart (art) and mind (knowledge)…and processes information from both the right hemisphere (emotion and intuition to see holistically) and left hemisphere (logic and sequence to see detail) of the brain. (p.408)

To further elaborate, cultural humility emphasizes the important balance of being client-centered while addressing the client holistically. This requires an art therapist to adhere to the client's depictions and needs of self while being aware of the interrelated aspects of the client that may also impact or be attributed to their lived experience. This may mean using traditional ways of addressing the client's needs while working in non-traditional ways of metaphors or practices that may be unfamiliar to the clinician. Jun stated, "The practitioner provides empathy and compassion…while searching through traditional and non-traditional therapeutic techniques" (2010, p.408). Many non-traditional practices encompass holistic exploration beginning with the body and the balance of the body, mind, and soul. The body as a way of knowing or the manifestation of self can make up a unique holistic form if given the acceptance to be unfiltered and detailed within its many natural nuances. Jun (2010) conveyed that "lack of self-judgment is key to reaching inner wisdom" (p.82), and that "listening to the body is another way to access inner experiences" (p.78). We must learn innately to "listen to their [our] bodies and increase their [our] awareness of their [our] inner experiences" (p.85). Seen through the balance of cultural humility, aspects felt or shown through the body such as "grace, beauty, and strength" can also appear "heavy, weighted, and weary, needing to take rest to rejuvenate" (Jackson, 2016).

## Compassion and compassion fatigue

In times of distress, confusion, and frustration it can be difficult to come forth with a culturally humble approach, developing into what is expressed as "compassion fatigue" or in the severity of trauma "vicarious trauma" (Hernández, Engstrom, & Gangsei, 2010). Due to this, self-critique and self-care become vital in the practice and "active concern for and care of self" (Martin & Barresi, 2008, p.261). Hernández *et al.* (2010, p.68) cited several authors who have explored the impact of trauma from various vantage points, thereby providing a multifaceted understanding of the processes by which the therapeutic relationship and the self of the therapist are influenced by traumatic material. Displaying a culturally humble stance in the therapeutic space, and otherwise, requires openness allowing vulnerability. This can be met with resistance, as this openness may expose the clinician to attack. And once having exposed oneself to the risk of confrontation, it may be difficult to continue with compassion. Hernández *et al.* (2010) cite Tedeschi and Calhoun in stating, "identified compassion and altruism as possible aspects of posttraumatic growth. These researchers posited that when people recognize their own vulnerability, they may be better able to feel compassion and that for this reason, the experience of trauma may act as a kind of empathy training" (p.69). This developed empathy training can then lead to acquiring strength attributes from clients who share stories of overcoming and withstanding in spite of tragedy, oppression, or trauma. This is described as reciprocity in vicarious resilience (Hernández *et al.*, 2010; Iqbal, 2015).

Cultural humility encourages a practitioner to acknowledge a client's strengths and used those strengths to empower the client. Many clients display resilience and have their own ability to journey through many obstacles with their own healing practices. Hernández *et al.* (2010) address the aspect of reciprocity in stating, "Reciprocity opens up the possibility of appreciating, attending to, and making meaning out of the process whereby therapists themselves may heal, learn, and change with clients" (p.73). Another aspect that relates to cultural humility is the awareness of those clients' multidimensional aspects and how they may have impacted their ability to foster resilience. After attending to the clients' multiple identities in the social context, they go on:

> Equally central is the therapist's ability to recognize her or his own multiple identities and the interaction of these identities with the client's in therapy. Hernández *et al.*, (2010) cite Brown in explaining, "It also requires the psychotherapist's awareness of her or his own identities, biases, and participation in cultural hierarchies of power and privilege, powerlessness and disadvantage, as well as personal experiences of trauma." (p.74)

In a training example, Hernández *et al.* (2010) asked questions such as:

> What challenges have you witnessed your clients overcoming in the therapeutic process? What did your client stimulate in you that you want to nurture and expand? Have any thoughts about how your perception of yourself may have been changed by your clients' resilience? Feel that your general outlook on the world has changed in some way? Identify any impact on your own views about spirituality? Have any thoughts about how your views on trauma work may have been positively impacted by your clients' resilience? Have any thoughts about how the ways you take care of yourself have been impacted by your clients' resilience? (p.78)

Lastly, related to the multifaceted aspects of one's identity, they asked: "If you were to consider that ethnicity, class, sexual orientation, religion, gender—theirs as well as your own—play a role in shaping your experience, how would they do so? (Engstrom, Hernández, &

Gangsei, 2008, p.22, as cited by Hernández *et al.*, 2010). The group responses offered a learning experience that allowed the therapist to respond to questions regarding "change in self-perception in relation to a client's resilience" (p.78). Witnessing a client's resilience can lead to a form of self-care if the therapist is willing to critically ask and self-examine hard questions about their therapeutic interactions with their clients.

Iqbal (2015) states that vicarious trauma "has been suggested to involve *'profound changes in the core aspect of the therapist's self'*" and "symptoms of vicarious traumatization can include *'a lack of empathy and trust towards others'*" (p.45). Again, this reinstates the importance of the self-reflective process in self-care. Iqbal says:

> Effective clinical work requires self-awareness on the part of the therapist. The ability to reflect on practice promotes self-awareness but also, within counseling psychology training, trainees are encouraged to reflect on their practice. Therefore, counseling psychologists may be better adjusted to work within the trauma field and distinguish the feelings, which belong to themselves and their clients. (p.48)

In supporting reciprocity and developing resilience from witnessing client's strength responses to trauma, Iqbal continues, "The ability to engage in self-care notably acknowledges that therapists are taking responsibility for themselves, and by taking responsibility, they may be aware of their clients' needs. Therefore, it is worthy to note vicarious resilience may support therapists in working ethically and professionally with clients" (p.49). The self-reflective process of cultural humility offers an engagement that displays a care for self and others as it offers a way to begin a proactive engagement with those we serve. This preventive course of action will allow for an art therapist to be responsive instead of reactive in the therapeutic space. Used as a form of preventative care, critical self-reflection will allow for a clinician to address symptoms like the pervasive presence of covert discrimination, microaggressions, and implicit bias (Brems & Rasmussen, 2019). Self-care is difficult to sustain if done alone, as there can be limitations to growth if not done in the presence and with the interrelated support of others. Brems and Rasmussen

(2019) say it is "necessary to help promote self-awareness through the presence of an outsider who is interested in the well-being and growth of the clinician" (p.55). This relates to the interpersonal communication that occurs when we interact with others. Having interpersonal relationships that allow for exchange and dialogue offers a validity check to process difficult aspects of self and avoid having the same assumptions, biases, and beliefs that may be a detriment to our way of knowing and relating to others.

In the divided and conflicted times of today, cultural humility can be a challenge for many. The world's strife, chaos, and confusion can lead one into a place of despair and hopelessness. Brems and Rasmussen (2019) say that some individuals have difficulty exploring and embracing diversity, "due to the fact that growing up in the United States has exposed them to a long history fraught with bias, stereotypes, and prejudice—often implicitly and automatically" (p.40). This is why having a culturally humble stance, modeled by art therapists for others, is so necessary in taking a stand against inequity and injustice while also leaving room for conversation and dialogue; doing so makes space for change to happen. Tillet and Tillet (2019) address self-care through the perspective of Black feminists. They relate self-care to activism as a form of preservation for Black women. In their work with teenage Black girls, they offer self-care as self-love, leading to advocacy and critical consciousness. This brings attention to the healing of the mind, body, and soul as a communal, interrelated aspect of self-care. Often, when we address the term self-care in our current social dynamics, it implies getting away from responsibility and social action. This marries into the privileged, Western ideology of self-care, where self-reflection becomes about being alone and becoming self-absorbed and indulgent. Self-care and reflection in cultural humility is done as a means to act in accordance with one's self and others. The self-reflective process of cultural humility offers balance, hope, and strength, based on possibilities. It shares the potential to have a dynamic shift in being and knowing. It offers a balance of approaching the therapeutic space and others with love and understanding as well as assertiveness and confidence. Cultural humility can relieve the pressure of competence, and instead encourage the practitioner to be a lifelong learner, "Clinicians forever asses their reactions to different situations and people in a continuous quest for personal growth and with everlasting humility that one will never truly arrive at a place of perfection" (Brems & Rasmussen, 2019, p.55). Being introspective with cultural humility requires one to be thoughtful and balanced in one's approach, considering what is said, what is put into the space and having mindfulness of self within that space. These efforts are not always meet with acceptance; resistance may ensue from others and self. In efforts to be culturally humble we must be compassionate to ourselves and others, show compassion for the art and the art process. There is no way around challenges, we must learn to be *with* the interrelatedness of being human and work *through* difficulties to learn and grow. Finding the balance is as relevant as the cycle of the butterfly and the photosynthesis process of the plant growing from a seed. It has to be nurtured and must go through struggles to grow and transform.

## REFLECTIVE PERSPECTIVE

### Reflection on Lifelong Process of Cultural Humility by Dr. Amy Backos

Respecting my scope of influence in the world allows me to attend in a very real and concrete way to cultural humility. My scope encompasses my family, friends, clients, co-workers, and students. The circle extends to all the people with whom they interact, and so on. I care deeply about these people in my life, but I also place value on their circle of influence, who are people I don't know and may never meet. My ability to stay present at dinner, in the office, and in class, matters not only to the people I am with and their circles of influence, and it matters to me as a way to have a meaningful life. I used to dramatically underestimate how much each of us impacts the wider world by each moment, alone or with others. In can feel like a lot of responsibility, but it is also reassuring that each interaction has meaning and purpose to benefit the future. This widening circle of influence and our interconnectedness is my current focus on cultural humility.

Students who recently talked to me about times where they experienced or witnessed a lack of cultural humility shared the insidious messages they got of "you do not belong." It was important to have the conversations and I felt sad about each of their experiences. One student reported being questioned by others about her disability in a way that was intrusive and invalidating, another about people oblivious to their white privilege, and the third was about her religion not being respected and looked upon as suspect. My reaction to hearing about these experiences includes immediate thoughts of "How can I fix this?" While fixing problems at work is often my job, my thought in these examples seemed to be a variation on the therapist fantasy of saving/fixing/curing someone. Students and emerging therapists often report these hero/heroine fantasies initially, but later suppress them when they learn that trying to save others is self-serving and often colonizing. I think it's better for me/us to keep recognizing these feelings and thoughts and use the them as information to get better at our work. Ignoring, suppressing, or immediately sublimating them fails because the feeling is likely to emerge again and perhaps be acted out unconsciously. Acting on another common feeling of wanting to "protect" someone who experienced religious discrimination or racism could be expressed in a patriarchal and patronizing manner. My discomfort with someone's negative experience, coupled with my frustration at systems that support the discrimination, might also lead to my own denial and minimization of their and my experiences.

When I am able to reflect and contain my immediate uncomfortable feelings that arise in conversations about privilege and racism, I can proceed without talking/acting in a way that serves only to relieve my own discomfort. If I can sit with the feeling and be curious to learn more, it nourishes my resolve to go deeper in my personal growth, and widens my circle of understanding about that person's experience. It is the wish to push away the discomfort or fix the problem that seems to bring me, and others, the most trouble. The willingness to linger with uncomfortable or unwanted feelings and accept what is happening in that situation has brought me the most peace in communication about culture and helped me move towards a stance of humility. I rely on these concepts from acceptance and commitment therapy to help keep me grounded in both my theoretical approach to my art therapy work and in my lifelong commitment to feminism and anti-racism.

"Do the best you can until you know better. Then when you know better, do better." This quote from Maya Angelou serves as my mantra when I am struggling through learning or transformation. I try to not be too hard on myself when I put my foot in my mouth, misunderstand a communication, exclude or ignore someone or something that needs attention. Self-compassion really seems to make all the difference in my ability to tolerate discomfort and stay with the person and/or situation long enough to make progress. If I am being challenged on my language/assumptions/attitude, I still have the urge to defend myself; but I do better when I can go slow and remind myself that a defensive position is a function of my ego being threatened, and I am not under threat in that moment. I learned much from watching others who communicate well in meaningful conversations. I can indeed be better with practice if I listen carefully, acknowledge my gaffe/offense/inattention, apologize or remedy if possible/appropriate, take responsibility for my own education/re-education, then reflect on the experience. In the same way I coach my clients recovering from addiction that a relapse/slip is not wasted if something can be learned from the experience, I can apply these principles to my own learning when communicating across cultures. I have also failed lots of times in confronting other white people, but I have had better success starting with "Are you open to having a conversation about this?"

I meditate most mornings and the 10 minutes of stillness to observe my thoughts truly helps me be patient in my interactions throughout the day. This is critical so I can be as present as possible and open to challenging myself and being challenged by others to attend to diversity. I find it vital that I keep educating/re-educating myself on issues of culture in my scholarly and academic work and I am committed to maintaining a circle of people who can support and challenge me. These things are necessary but they are not sufficient—the willingness to tolerate my own uncomfortable emotions allows the work to really sink in and become congruent with my values.

## RESPONSE ART

*Figure 6.3 A. Backos "Inside Outside." Media & materials: crochet with recycled fabric, embroidery thread, a plastic bead*

## REFLECTIVE EXERCISE F: **INTEGRATION OF THE WHOLE**

Often art therapists use metaphor to help conceptualize treatment. The mind, body, and soul metaphor was developed to help metaphorically structure a cultural considerations art therapy Master's course (Bodlovic & Jackson, 2018). The three aspects are linked to three of the cultural humility tenets: (1) lifelong learning and critical self-reflections; (2) recognizing and challenging power imbalance for respectful partnerships; and (3) developing mutually beneficial and non-paternalistic clinical and advocacy partnerships with communities on behalf of individuals and defined populations (Bodlovic & Jackson, 2018, p.3).

■ **Goal:** To self-reflect through the depiction of the multidimensional/ multilayered intersectionality of self-identity.

■ **Materials:** Previously done artwork, paper, markers, pencils, crayons, color paper, scissors and glue, collage images, and model magic, yarn and other decorative items, paint, watercolor, tissue paper and fabric.

■ **Prompt:** Holistic self-reflective art piece.

1. Mind: Examine the systems that impact the ways we think about others, the world, ourselves. Create a piece of art using structured materials (paper, markers, pencils, crayons, colored paper, scissors and glue, collage images) to depict your mind construct.

   Reflect on concepts such as colonialism, racism, classism, sexism, heteronormativism and ableism.

   Explore your relationship to these concepts.

2. Body: Examine how we personally move through the above-mentioned systems to form our identities.

   Examine the ways people band together and the rituals we use to make sense of the world, such as rituals related to family, politics, spirituality, and illness.

   Using more fluid materials (model magic, yarn, and other decorative items, fabric) create a piece of art focusing on learning through encounters with others.

3. Spirit: Examine cultural celebrations that bring communities together and the roles of therapist and activist in communities.

   Reflect on the commitment of cultural humility while focusing on the strength of the communities we are a part of.

   Explore how you might illuminate the spark inside of you that connects and communicates to others and communities.

   Create a piece of art that depicts this spark using fluid materials (tissue paper, paint, and watercolor).

4. Integration of the whole: Explore the aspects of self that would develop into a culturally humble art therapist.

   Examine the three art pieces that depict mind, body, and spirit in relationship to each other.

   Using these art pieces consciously integrate your aspects of identity that will solidify your meaning of a culturally humble art therapist.

   Add to the final piece things that maybe missing that you are working on or want to include.

5. Using written reflections done through this book or other journal writings, write a paragraph using holistic statements, I statements, positive affirmations.

6. Share the piece, reading the statement out loud, then dialogue about the importance of the whole person.

CHAPTER 7

# Cultural Humility in Pedagogy

*Symbols: Making Meaning, Developing Metaphor,*
*Placing Cultural Humility in Context and Meaning*

*Figure 7.1 Collective Study Collaborator Art 001*

## Addressing diversity concerns in education and clinical art therapy

Issues in educational and clinical art therapy settings continue to arise in areas such as lack of multicultural education and cultural competence, lack of research and training for educators, and lack of diversity within the profession (Calisch, 2003). In the article "Ethical dilemmas in multicultural counseling," Sadgehi *et al.* (2003, p.180) state, "although recent efforts have been made, there is a paucity of ethics education material for counselors regarding multicultural issues. This lack of multicultural ethical training suggests a need to develop multicultural ethics education materials for counselors." Recognizing the power differential in the therapeutic relationship requires taking this discussion into the classroom where the study of diversity is a "palimpsest on which fresh narratives about equity can take shape—before students go out to work with clients" (George *et al.*, 2005, p.137). Furthermore, art therapy training needs to implore students to understand "their identities in relationship to systems of domination and dehumanization" (Gipson, 2015, p.142), while asking them to examine their own racial and ethnic biases, in order to become culturally humble art therapists (Calish, 2003).

Once I discovered cultural humility, I felt it was my responsibility to share it with the institutions I was working in, beginning with the county where my training with the principles began. There I would share *Stories with a Heart*, an account of creative endeavors that used art as a way to express advocacy and the principles of cultural humility. The three projects were Digital Story Telling (The Center for Digital Storytelling, Berkeley, CA), Reachout.com video interpretations (Inspire USA Foundation & Bay Area Video Coalition [BAVC]), and Photovoice (Youth Leadership Institute). After offering presentations in many different disciplines and spaces, I recognize the accountability in bringing both art therapy and cultural humility into places where there was little knowledge of either. This effort would illuminate the lack of cultural considerations in some areas and highlight the work that was being done in others. After the county, I would have the opportunity to bring art therapy and cultural humility into university settings. There I would teach, present, assess, and implement curricula in support of both practices and theory. I was able to address the cultural humility principle of "advocating for and maintaining institutional accountability" (Tervalon & Lewis, 2018). The accountability came with considerable responsibility that would be further illuminated as I engaged in teaching my first co-facilitated cultural considerations course in a university art therapy program.

In the marital and family therapy program, which specializes in art therapy, two professors had facilitated the Cultural Considerations in Art Therapy course for a number of years. This would be the first time Anthony Bodlovic and I would teach the class together. It would also be the first time we met each other. Strongly standing by the principles of cultural humility in which I was practicing for many years, I shared my desire to incorporate the principles into our course. Anthony, being receptive and supportive of the ideas, sought to learn and implement the principles further. After our first run at the course, we realized upon evaluation that we had cultivated a curriculum that depicted the metaphors of mind, body, and soul (Bodlovic & Jackson, 2018). Through our experience with co-teaching with one another, we have been able to develop a mutual respect and an appreciation that has led to a model in teaching this course. This model again included the principles of cultural humility, along with the three components of bias, assumptions, and belief, depicted through mind, body, and soul.

After teaching the class a second time, we refined many areas, making the class more consolidated, with clear intention. With the holistic practice of using the themes we addressed the previous year, we offered the students an experience that was enlightening and challenging. After reviewing our syllabi together, we restructured the themes to align with the model designed for the class while being mindful of the level of engagement into cultural issues perceived by the students. At this time we also looked at our assignments and altered them to be less cumbersome and more of an effective learning tool. Throughout the semester we continued to learn from the students and restructured our classes to offer shorter, more directed lectures and presentations, time to reflect through the art, and an opportunity at the end of class for the students to have small group dialogues. The students had asked to have more time to process and to share through dialogue the, at times, new and overwhelming material. The restructuring also allowed us to define three assignments that went along with the model for the class (Bodlovic & Jackson, 2018). We began with cultural engagements to exercise the concept of cultural biases, then case consultation to illustrate the awareness of assumptions, ending the course with a cultural journal that encapsulates the entire class experience as a way of representing old and new beliefs. This enriched our course methodology and led to meeting some of our goals from the previous year. With each subsequent year, we continued to re-evaluate and expand on our class, developing further endeavors into scholarship. The facilitation of this course has spawned collaborative developments such as conference presentations, facilitating a workshop sharing our partnership with the course and the innovative and dynamic aspects we incorporated to encourage cultural awareness in art therapy pedagogy and practice, research and collective academic writing generated from a pilot study identifying goals and challenges of collaborative pedagogy of cultural considerations in art therapy.

As this class journey has continued to spark accountability within the institution we work in, the use of teaching has also enhanced my research and creative work through a few different collaborative and individual endeavors. One is a workshop presentation developed for the AATA 2017 conference, where Anthony Bodlovic and I presented a collaborative workshop on diversity pedagogy in art therapy based on our Cultural Considerations in Marital and Family Arts Psychotherapy class. The workshop focused on using cultural humility as a framework to educate on cultural issues in arts psychotherapy. The workshop guided participants through hands-on art directives that were utilized in our course. Attendees were assisted in identifying the components of cultural humility and aspects of cultural identity that may surface in the classroom, to implement various arts-based teaching strategies to address a variety of complex issues related to diversity and culture, and in creative self-reflective work that will help students identify their own biases and obstacles to compassion, utilizing a holistic approach. The future sustainability of the above-mentioned scholarship/creative works and clinical leadership has evolved through other collaborative opportunities, such as an acquired Faculty Incentive Grant (FIG), an external grant that is being used to foster a pilot study to collect data and research the co-teaching of cultural issues and diversity in art therapy. The pilot study is exploring how diversity training for Master's-level students can be implemented in art therapy and related health fields with the concept of cultural humility and art. It consists of traveling to programs where students are assigned practicum sites in the greater Los Angeles County areas to offer training in cultural considerations in art therapy. Research data will be collected to further support pedagogical practices and develop training theories that could be used for instructional literature and interdisciplinary publication and collaboration. The training would model the structure of our Cultural Issues in Marital and Family Arts Psychotherapy class.

This work has been expanded further to include cultural humility trainer training, where we were trained as facilitators and will be able to offer training in the Marital and Family Therapy Department and the university community. Doby-Copeland (2006a) suggests "art therapists endeavoring to teach cultural diversity courses without having been trained to do so are engaging in unethical practices" (p.174). The collaborative model also gained our acceptance to present in the 8th International Conference on Diversity in Organizations, Communities & Nations, the University of Texas at Austin, June 2018. Our presentation title "Cultural humility in collaborative art therapy pedagogy" used the art materials acquired through the FIG grant to again pilot our model. In addition, we were asked to submit an article to the peer-reviewed journal, *The International Journal of Diversity in Education*, titled, "A cultural humility approach to art therapy multicultural pedagogy: barriers to compassion" (Bodlovic & Jackson, 2018). Recognizing the importance of social awareness, diversity education, and self-reflection, this article introduces the development and execution of the multicultural co-facilitation of an art therapy Master's-level diversity course. We presented the course in detail, beginning with the dynamics of multicultural co-instruction, which became the strength of the course. This was followed by an overview of the tools, techniques, theories, and practices that instructors made available to engage students in the holistic approach of cultural humility when applied to art therapy practice. Art directives were discussed to demonstrate directives used within the course. Although many benefits are discussed, the article concludes with the reporting of challenges, recognition, and conclusions.

Through our efforts to bring a cultural humble approach to our department within our university, many wonderful things have emerged as well as struggles and challenges. It became apparent very early that students felt invigorated and hopeful with the appearance of a new, full-time faculty of color, the first in the department's history. As students of color began to feel safety in using their voice, comments of feeling isolated, misunderstood, and exploited began to surface. A student spoke about feeling invisible and taken advantage of. Others spoke of feeling appreciative that there now was a full-time faculty of color. Potash *et al.* (2015) supports this dynamic: "Art therapists and students of diverse racial, social, and cultural identities independently and spontaneously seek each other out to promote visibility and advocacy, as well as to inform, mentor, support, and celebrate one another" (p.148). The department accepted my suggestion to hold community meetings that would offer a collective space for the entire department to convene together to dialogue about these and other concerns, as well as inform and celebrate each other. It was during the first of these meetings that the first comments of feeling silenced and appreciation were put into the space.

With this opportunity also came challenges, reflection and response as the department was guided into institutional accountability, again, the fourth principle of cultural humility. Following the community meeting space, the cultural competence committee was forming and moved into a name change, calling themselves the Active Community Explorations (ACE) Committee, recognizing they were not just there to make cultural considerations to the department but to also offer a place for students, faculty, and alumni to engage and for educated cultural exchanges within and outside of the department. The ACE committee hosted the first social commons, a space where those who shared common cultural variables could join and reflect on their lived experience and share with others. The first community commons was directed to students and art therapists of color. With the low percentage of professors and supervisors of color in predominately white institutions, not only can students feel isolated, alumni can as well, as the same demographics hold true in the field (Potash *et al.*, 2015). The discussion of intersectionality was engaged through literature as a foundation, art as a depiction and vehicle, and dialogue as a way to share stories of lived experience and future endeavors. Many appreciated the space, shared similar struggles, and referred to the community commons as a place of hope in art.

Another implementation in the department has been training on cultural humility and the idea of dialogue amongst students and faculty. The space was offered first to the students and faculty, then alumni, and then faculty and supervisors. It was recognized that this would not be a "safe" space after students expressed the need to feel safe. The discussions of having the privilege to express one's thoughts and feelings and have them validated in a "safe space" and requiring that "safe space" in order to speak, is a privilege that not everyone is allowed. It was then presented that the space would be a critically comfortable space relating to the critical self-evaluation that is a part of cultural humility. Modeled by my co-facilitator Anthony Bodlovic and myself, we expressed vulnerability and the usage of "oops and ouches" (Tervalon & Lewis, 2018). Being able to humbly acknowledge when we may have stung someone or listen when someone expresses how they may have felt stung is a way to take accountability and become our best selves, people, art therapists, and community.

Because we modeled this and included ourselves in this, a student, following this discussion, wrote to me about her admiration and viewing me as a mentor, and then expressed how she had been "ouched" by me in class. Although at first it was uncomfortable, as some students may fall back onto being "ouched" when given critical feedback in class, it also allowed me to hear a student's concern and address it in a culturally humble manner. The student was able to express a need and I was able to take accountability for the exchange that took place in the class that could have potentially harmed a student. Other students from other classes have since come to me in private to expressed feeling "ouched." When a conversation in class included tattoos, a student expressed feeling that the class and myself looked at her, giving her a feeling of being judged. After being responded to in a culturally humble manner where the student was acknowledged, heard, and encouraged to use their voice when they felt it appropriate, this student shared their concerns with the class. In a culturally humble manner, the student used a future assignment on sub-cultures to share with the class medical journal articles that both informed and stigmatized those with tattoos. The student took the opportunity in class to discuss the judgment they had felt from clients, client's families, and peers based on their body modifications. Another student mentioned being "ouched" by the use of the word "powwow," sharing that the use of the word by the professors in the class may display a misappropriation for the term and minimize the importance of it to the indigenous people of this country. The aspect of "oops and ouch" is a way to take accountability for our actions when we have misstepped or caused a microaggression against others. A way to respond to this is encouraging the expression on needs. At the time of our community forum, feelings of "needs" were shared as a way to design a path forward. Stating our needs, similar to a process of non-violent communications, allows for a response that comes from the value of the relationship in order to offer a request for change or action that is not perceived as aggressive (Rosenberg, 2003). Once a need is expressed it is then important to take accountability for actions one can take to get those needs met. Expressing a need to others allows for reparations to take place. In conjunction to that, and just as imperative, is the necessity for the person expressing the need to self-examine how they might also take accountability by addressing the need themselves. When engaging in a needs assessment, it is important to express the need with an "I" statement—asserting that there has been a self-exploration in which the need was derived. The act of accountability becomes strong when a self-examination can express movements or steps that can shift towards meeting some of these needs. In other words, evolving past what I need to, to what can I do, to get those needs met. The final action is to be careful to not get attached to our needs, as room must be left for transformation or change. After closing the dialogue during the community gathering, the principles of cultural humility were then placed in the student handbook and they are now reviewed by the students as a community every semester.

There are many challenges and struggles for students when desiring to comprehend and use a culturally humble approach. Students of color at times have felt that a more direct and hard approach was needed to create change and to be heard. They were encouraged to share their lived experience and their voices without sacrificing their self-respect, meaning to reframe from attacking, using profane language, and cutting off dialogue. Their anger and frustration were understood and, although changes were taking place, it became apparent that these changes were not being implemented or practiced in some of the spaces they were encountering, whether in the department, university, or in the community while providing services. There were other students who identified as feeling shut down by empowered students of color who were recognizing their voices and expressing them. Professors can exert oppression when they express the need for students of color to be careful (not expressive) when sharing their cultural experiences. This request can be due to the professor's lack of humility or fear of how to respond. Professors will praise non-colored students for their appropriate sharing of cultural issues, while not being aware that students of color have been institutionalized into muffling their voices to create a sense of safety and comfort for others. Once they find and use their voices, most are passionate in their expression, due to oppression being a current reality and lived experience. This can also leave them open to micro-aggressions from other students of privilege who may not have compassion for those whose lives are constantly subjugated.

There are professors that add to their syllabi that they are incorporating culture into their class. It is important to name specifically what "culture" means. Because culture is broad and encompasses many aspects of identity, students may misconstrue what is meant and have a different expectation than the professor intended. Culture can mean the culture of art therapy in general. It could mean diverse populations with practice defined through diagnosis and setting. When relating to cultural humility and the identities of self, such as race, ethnicity, religion, gender, sexuality, ability, region, and so on, this should be clearly identified. Doby-Copeland (2006a) shares that, "Clarifying terminology is fundamental to developing the program philosophy" (p.173). If professors find themselves uncomfortable with the topic of culture, as defined previously, in the space of other besides the dominant culture, then the professor should name that in the space and avoid cutting off or dismissing the topic when students of color share their lived experiences.

## Cultural humility challenges and objectives in pedagogy

I, in turn, had my own challenges while making efforts to bring cultural humility into a department as a way to support institutional accountability. Being a woman of color in a homogeneous environment has been a lifelong challenge in many of my educational and clinical experiences. This in itself brings about struggle. I was challenged with finding balance while dealing with being heard through my intersectionality as a woman of color, art therapist, and newly hired full-time tenure-track professor, while holding the space and conversation of culture within the department and beyond. I felt compelled in many directions including to support students of color, all students, faculty, the department, the university, alumni, and the field. This is echoed by Gipson (2015), who conveys:

> By bringing my own narratives into the classroom, I have invited students to engage perspectives of difference and question dominant discourse. Each time, talking about issues of race from my perspective as a Black woman, I have opened myself to risks of being confronted with accusations of belaboring the point or "playing the race card." Instead of engaging in the process of learning, some White students have felt silenced by my voice in the classroom. Students are not to blame for this structural problem. Art therapy has, by and large, excluded from its history and curriculum the legacy of art therapists of color. (Gipson, 2015, p.144)

Paulo Freire, a Brazilian educator and activist, addressed the concepts, which have influenced my approach to teaching, in his book *Pedagogy of the Oppressed* (1970). He spoke about educating the people by working with the people, addressing their needs, and allowing them to participate in the process. He brought about the idea of learning with, instead of teaching at. Helguera (2011), addresses the concept of collaboration in socially engaged art (SEA), where he states how "Freire directly acknowledged the differences of knowledge and experience between himself" and the 300 sugarcane workers he taught to read in 45 days (pp.51–52). Through a game of questioning, Helguera (2011) shares how Freire realized that the difference of the knowledge between him and the farmers "did not denote superior intelligence on either side, but instead was connected to the difference in their environments, interests, and access to various opportunities" (p.52). Students may not be depicted as "oppressed," but it is acknowledged that their lack of advanced education and experience does not mean they do not have something to contribute to their educational journey. They are the experts in their own understanding. Helguera continues by referencing the concept of "expert," which is also addressed by Levine and Levine (2011) who refer to McNiff (1993) in stating that, "the role of 'expert' should not be exclusively claimed by the therapist or even by the clients or community, but the role of 'expert' should be shared through the very experience of creating and the very image that arises in the work" (p.47). Although McNiff (1993) does not reference teachers, in my belief of pedagogy I believe sharing experience through creation applies equally. The foundations of Freire's work resonate with the founding principles of cultural humility, such as working with others and communities, addressing the power imbalance, and seeing others as experts to their own lived experience and institutional accountability.

My objective as a teacher is to create an environment that allows the opportunity for students to become experts of their experiences. This is fostered through the principles of cultural humility and a strengths-based approach. I encourage students to acknowledge and learn from their strengths through real-world application and continuous self-reflection. While teaching and acknowledging the importance of knowing foundations and history, such as being able to discuss and apply theory, innovative thinking is also encouraged.

I believe art to be an integrated experience that can acknowledge other ways of knowing. My intentions in class are to demonstrate integrated art experiences through collective art projects. I initiate my classes with the validation of open discussion and collective dialogue. This encourages the inquisitive nature of students and supports the practice of respectful inquiry, one of the concepts of cultural humility. I believe that curiosity sparks creativity. Suggesting "a cultural discovery approach, where the art therapist taps into the client's life experiences to aid in the therapeutic process" is shared by Doby-Copeland (2006a, p.176).

As a teacher, I subscribe to the notion that one of my roles is to challenge creative thinking and responsibility. One of these responsibilities is the understanding and acknowledgment of one's own bias and beliefs, whether student or teacher. I offer self-reflection by including digital media and art. Students are encouraged to know who they are as it applies to their history, experience, and worldview. An aspect of cultural humility is to engage in honest self-reflection about your social and cultural identity (Tervalon, 2015). This is done in class through response art, acknowledgment of countertransference, maintaining a personal art-making practice, and collaboration of practice with the community. I ask students to share and teach directives they are using with their specific populations with the class to encourage diverse and collective learning. Small group learning is also implemented to support collaborative and interactive teaching among students. These approaches assist students with various ways of learning and knowing. Students receive frequent verbal and/or written comments on their performance in class. Examples from my personal experiences are often used to illustrate points about the material presented and what is being discussed in class. Sharing my knowledge and expertise with students is very important to me. I guide students' work on course projects by asking questions, exploring options, and suggesting alternatives. I spend time consulting with students on how to improve their work on individual and/or group projects. Learning from the students has been effective in measuring whether the objectives I established in the class have been met. Directly asking students collectively and independently for their feedback on their teaching experience has allowed me to reflect and refine my teaching methods. Students are also asked to digitally capture their class experience through art, theory, practice, and reflections. The digital video becomes a way to evaluate their application of what they have learned in class. Students are also encouraged to demonstrate their knowledge of class with real-life experience and practice through written and oral presentation. This beneficial flow of dialogue with students creates a culturally humble stance for me as a teacher and allows the students to be the experts in their learning experience, fostering a strong culturally humble art therapist identity.

The final video project for the students in Adolescent Psychotherapy is introduced using the framing of Bolman and Deal (2008). They describe a frame as encompassing all the images that capture part of an idea we want to convey such as maps, tools, lenses, orientation filters, prisms and perspectives and that "A good frame makes it easier to know what you are up against and ultimately, what you can do about it" (p.11). The authors state that a frame is a mental model that includes a set of ideas, assumptions, and judgments we make based on the information we have at hand, our mental map, and how well we use them. They state that a good map helps you navigate the specific environment you are in and helps you to stay with that journey. In association with the video, I convey to the students that this video is meant to assist them in developing their frame in navigating working with adolescents. Because this time of development, both for the adolescent and the student in their adolescence in becoming clinicians, is multilayered, the video allows for them to take "a complicated and uncertain environment" and simplify it by developing "better systems and technology to collect and process information" (Bolman & Deal, 2008, p.36). To support the importance of critical self-reflection in cultural humility, Bolman and Deal state, "Since our interpretations depend so much on our cognitive repertoires, expectations, beliefs and values, our internal world is as important as what is outside—sometimes more so" (p.38). Because adolescence in development and clinical development can be confusing it is crucial for students at this phase to examine their bias, assumptions, and beliefs while in the midst of developing their confidence. This means challenging motivations for our actions in practice and recognizing our mistakes. The video allows the students to engage in this critical self-examination in the environment of the classroom as opposed to in therapeutic engagement with a client. Bolman and Deal (2008) share this in conveying, "This learning needs to happen before we find ourselves in make-or-break situations" and that "holding on to old patterns is ineffective…even if we see no flaws in our current mindset, because our theories are self-sealing filters—they block us from recognizing our errors" (p.39).

This engagement can be challenging for some students who rationalize their one-lens frames. Bolman and Deal (2008) state, "Extensive research documents the many ways in which individuals spin reality to protect existing beliefs" (pp.39–40). Most students in our program identify as white female and appear to be from regions in the country that are only exposed to, and align with, Western culture and ideology. Although many are open and shift their perspectives with the engagement in the program, self-examination to include a multilayered approach can feel overwhelming and confusing. The influence of Western culture is echoed by Bolman and Deal (2008):

> In Western cultures, particularly, there is a tendency to embrace one theory or ideology and to try to make the world conform. If it works we persist in our view. If discrepancies arise, we try to rationalize them away. If people challenge our view, we ignore them or out them in their place (p.40)

Being able to engage in the video presentation allows for the students to use an assortment of lenses where each client in a therapeutic engagement can tell their own story. As a developing clinician "the ability to shift nimbly from one to another helps redefine situations so they become understandable and manageable…the intuitive capacity to use them with skill and grace, it is a world of excitement and possibility" (p.41).

Before engaging in the video project, the students are given a rubric, which includes four content areas: clinical, biological, historical, and culture. These four content areas align with Bolman and Deal's (2008) Four-Frame Model: structural, human resources, historical, and symbolic. I convey to the students, using the charts from the book, that the central concepts of the Four-Frame Model offer a multilayer lens guideline with clinical reflecting rules, roles, goals, policies, technology and environment; biology reflecting family, needs, skills, relationships; historical reflecting power, conflict, competition, and organizational politics (macro and micro social/political constructs); and culture reflecting meaning, metaphor, ritual, ceremony, stories, heroes/heroines (Bolman & Deal, 2008, p.18). All of these areas offer a rich perspective that lends to a culturally humble approach in self-reflecting and awareness. We also discuss the barriers to change in each content area, as we look at the adolescent and the feelings they maybe currently experiencing as they are in their adolescent phase in the program: feelings such as lack of direction, confusion, anxiety, uncertainty, incompetence, needy, disempowered, conflict, loss of meaning and purpose, and clingy to the past (p.379).

As we close the discussion of the final video project, I dialogue with the students the importance of sharing the video with the class as a way to challenge our narratives by receiving feedback and openly displaying our new-found awareness, or lack thereof, to others in an environment that is practicing being culturally humble while offering a critical comfortable space. Our intra-dialogue can be self-validating by continually rationalizing our skewed bias, assumptions and beliefs, which can perpetuate our actions. It is not until we engage in interpersonal dialogue that we receive the feedback loop necessary to critically examine our thought patterns. To balance the insecurity that may come from this understanding, I share with the students a quote from Bolman and Deal that can offer a strengths-based approach, moving them into the hopefulness of leadership:

> Artists interpret experience and express it in forms that can be felt, understood, and appreciated by others. Art embraces emotion, subtlety, ambiguity. An artist reframes the world so others can see new possibilities. Modern organizations often rely too much on engineering and too little on art in searching for quality, commitment, and creativity. Art is not a replacement for engineering but an enhancement. Artistic leaders and managers help us look beyond today's reality to new forms that release untapped individual

energies and improve collective performance. The leader as artist relies on images as well as memos, poetry as well as policy, reflection as well as command, and reframing as well as refitting. (Bolman & Deal, 2008, p.21)

I convey to the students that, in their development to becoming effective, culturally humble, clinicians, they will experience challenges and many successes. In our discussion of the quote, we dialogue about the students being the "artistic leaders." And that through the development of a multilayered lens, they are expanding their intuitiveness to reach new epistemology and ways of knowing themselves and those they engage with. This requires not only having the experience of the power of the art, they also have to integrate their learning of theoretical application and clinical practice. I share with them that, just as in getting new glasses, sometimes the lens offers a good view of the environment and all we need is to make some adjustments to the frame. Other times it is not just the frame, it is also the fitting of a new lens. Growth in cultural humility requires examining our old ways of knowing and experiencing, and evolving by continually learning and critically self-examining.

## The wonders of teaching

Being able to offer myself for support and encouragement has increased my awareness of pedagogy. Teaching can be an environment of coaching, motivation, and advocacy, while also offering discipline, limit setting, and boundaries, so as to not encourage learned helplessness. I want students to be as effective as they can be, but ultimately it is their responsibility. I will bring in the tools that are necessary and offer the appropriate materials.

I try to embody cultural humility as a way to teach and model the concept. My goal is to achieve this by implementing cultural humility constructively into art therapy education through research and development. A specific goal for myself as a teacher is to further develop a focus on cultural humility in art therapy and strengthen my skill in pedagogy. My future goal is to design a method of implementing cultural humility with art therapy education programs, including faculty, students, and clients (community) to enact equity amongst diverse populations served and those providing the services.

By engaging in cultural humility as a lifelong practice I am opening my self and my students to self-discovery and the education of the whole person. Together with academic excellence students are becoming aware of their role in integrating openly with the communities where they work and live, and worldwide to advocate intercultural learning. As my career in teaching is in the early stages, I am willing to open myself to the vast knowledge and experiences I have yet to accumulate. On this journey, I will have the opportunity to alter, reconstruct, or integrate my philosophy of pedagogy. The fascinating thing about education is that is it fluid and ever-changing, similar to cultural humility. Currently, I am enjoying traveling on this journey as both a student and a teacher. My goal is to continue as a lifelong student, learning from my experiences and those I share those experiences with.

The institutional accountability that comes with being a culturally humble art therapist and professor/educator does not only apply to the institution we work in but also to our larger organizations such as the AATA. Early pioneers challenged the AATA and the field of art therapy to become less exclusive (Venture, 1977). I think this becomes relevant when we hold our institutions accountable in the cultural humility principles of critically self-reflecting and engaging in mutually beneficial relationships on behalf of communities and those they serve. It is necessary to hold them accountable for addressing power imbalance through nominating diverse individuals into the organization and hiring within our universities and teaching establishments. In a recent thesis study, a self-survey recognized that many alumni regarded their former professors as having the most influence over their identity as an art therapist. As institutions and organizations critically reflect on matters of diversity, equity, and inclusion, recognizing the impact the faculty, supervisors, committees, and boards have through their visual and structural make-up is paramount. This requires not only advocating for justice, it also means becoming part of these institutions and organizations and creating change from within. When asked to be nominated for the 2019 AATA board, I was surprised and a little disenchanted. Although I had been intermittently involved in my local AATA chapter, I had kept my distance from the national organization. For one, I thought it was too expensive, with little reciprocity, and felt no connection to its membership as it appeared to cater to largely white middle-class and older women. However, I quickly understood from the invitation that there was a need for me to be on the board. I took this as a call for continued action and change, and answered it. Recognizing that talking and writing about the need for change was important and that taking a role within to shift power imbalance was equally detrimental, if not more so, I spoke using the cultural humility principles in which I am trained, which may have resonated with others, as I was voted into the executive board. When pounding on a door or shouting outside, those inside may be less likely to offer an invitation to come in and hear concerns. Using culturally humble dialogue can allow trust within an organization, to be welcomed in and have a seat at the table, which allows the institution to welcome new epistemology, ideas, and integrations into art therapy. This approach may not always be effective and one may have to demand a seat at the table as a right. I was blessed and honored to have had art therapy teachers like Dr. Doris Arrington, who, from the onset of entering the field, made it clear and direct that having more diversity, such as myself as a Black woman, was needed in the field. From there I continued to gain support from other professors at Notre Dame de Namur University (Dr. Carolan, Dr. Etherington, Dr. Backos, Dr. Sanders) who were willing to support my efforts to shift the power imbalance and become agents for change. This was increased by Dr. Linesh, who, hearing my response to a question at a conference presentation where we were introduced by faculty from NDNU, encouraged me to apply for a tenure faculty position at Loyola Marymount University. Now in position there, I continue to receive support from the faculty and university in my effort to bring diversity, equity, and inclusion to the field of art therapy with the principles of cultural humility. Cultural humility offers the tools needed when in dialogue to make advances for social change with institutions, associations, universities, communities, those we serve, and students.

## REFLECTIVE PERSPECTIVE

### Personal Perspective by Anthony Bodlovic

One of my father's favorite stories to tell was the first time he took us to Disneyland. To my father this iconic theme park was more than just an entertainment destination—it was a symbol of everything my parents left Croatia for, a symbol of American ideals and ingenuity made manifest in foam, paint, and mechanical wonders. The part of the story I'm concerned with doesn't take place in the spectacle of Disneyland's various lands and attractions, but in a souvenir shop near the exit of the park. My father, overcome with joy, proclaimed that I could purchase anything in the store, anything I wanted. He quickly realized the implications of his wording when I began to peruse overstuffed and overpriced jungle animals and precious porcelain figurines, which were individually numbered for the benefit of collectors. To his relief, and surprise, I came back with a modest, hardcover, children's book. At the conclusion of his tale the guests who were listening would chuckle in amazement, or let out a touching "awe," but regardless they would all turn to me with loving approval. My father tells this story to entertain, but also to explain how early on he knew I would be an academic. Throughout my life I would wonder why I actually chose that book. Was it true, like my father tells it, I was predestined to love literature and the arts? But I also wonder if my choice was less of an omen, and the reason I learned to love to read was because I wanted to be the boy in my father's story he was so proud of.

Narratives have always occupied my imagination and many of my artistic pursuits. The stories I tend to gravitate to are typically about underdogs, psychopomps, and lands between lands. Looking retrospectively, I can see how these stories mirrored my own lived experiences. Being Croatian, American, and queer, I find myself often existing in liminal spaces. I always felt like an American in Croatia, and a Croatian in America. Perhaps somewhere over the Atlantic was where I would find myself. I felt caught between cultures, between tongues, and as my sexuality developed, caught between society's expectations and my own internal feelings. These stories spoke to me because they were, in fact, my own.

When I met Dr. Louvenia Jackson I learned another story, the story of cultural humility. She brought in a narrative that helped me find language to navigate through the in-between spaces that are within and outside of me. The space between two people is vast, with an ocean of experiences between them. The tenets of cultural humility as outlined by Dr. Melanie Tervalon and Dr. Jann Murray Garcia provided tools on how to cross that ocean. Naming cultural humility as a lifelong process with no end helped give language to a process it took me a long time to find on my own, emphasizing there is no destination—I can be this *and* that, Queer *and* Croatian, here *and* there. The tenets as a teaching tool provided a structure to hold the information I have gathered through years of multicultural education, placed it in a framework that allows for dialogue and accountability. They offer a model of how to be not just a thoughtful clinician, but how to thoughtfully BE. Once I understood those tenets, I knew I wanted to be a person in that story.

## RESPONSE ART

With humility, my eyes see the kaleidescope of my heart. I honor the prisms of color, light and shadow surrounding each of us.

Love and peace nourish my soul.
I quietly listen to each speaker as wise

Melanie Terralon
4/2016

*Figure 7.2 Collective Study Collaborator Art 018*

## REFLECTIVE EXERCISE G: **HOLDING SPACE—BAG/VESSEL/CONTAINER**

■ **Goal:** Through our engagement in this class, Anthony and I have forged a dedication to cultural humility and mutual respect for one another. After dialoguing about the training, presentations, and writings regarding our experience of the class, we made revisions. We streamlined some of our in-class presentations to allow for more small-group dialogue amongst the students, which was one of the things asked for in our student evaluations. We also condensed some of our art directives and incorporated them into one ongoing art project; a vessel, bag, or container. This "bag" seemed to hold the student's experience of the class in a tangible and depictable manner. It offered a place to examine biases, assumptions, and beliefs as well as alter and constantly interact with them throughout the course.

We also revised our final project, making the former hands-on project into a digital format. Although some of the artistic creativity was lost, the concrete format may have developed more cohesion for the students. The creative liberties that were needed to synthesize the at times dense and overwhelming material were then transferred to their created "bag."

■ **Materials:** Variety of structured and instructed materials.

■ **Prompt:**

1. Using chosen materials construct a vessel/bag/container.

   The bag should depict parts of your identity and depiction of self.

   It may also incorporate symbols that relate to different aspects of identity.

   Keep the bag accessible as you journey through self-reflection.

2. When a bias, assumption, or belief is discovered, alter the "bag" to depict that change.

   It may require you to add, remove, or place inside of the bag.

3. Periodically, examine the bag.

   Explore what concepts have shifted, solidified, altered, or been removed.

   Journal in conjunction with the bag to capture the moments and expressions of change.

# References

Abdul-Raheem, J. (2018) Cultural humility in nursing education. *Journal of Cultural Diversity, 25*(2), 66–73.

Acton, D. (2001) The "color blind therapist." *Art Therapy: Journal of the American Art Therapy Association, 18*(2), 109–112.

Adichie, C. (2009) The danger of a single story. Accessed on 08/26/2019 at www.ted.com/talks/chimamanda_adichie_the_danger_of_a_single_story.

Africa, J., & Endres, A. (2009) Towards better quality of care: applying the cultural competence and cultural humility to our daily work. Accessed on 08/23/2019 at www.smchealth.org/sites/main/files/file-attachments/caminarhandout0509.pdf.

Allen, P.B. (2008) Commentary on community-based art studios: underlying principles. *Art Therapy: Journal of the American Art Therapy Association, 25*(1), 11–12.

American Art Therapy Association (2004) *Ethical Principles for Art Therapists.* Mundelein, IL: AATA.

American Art Therapy Association (2013) *Ethical Principles for Art Therapists.* Mundelein, IL: AATA.

American Counseling Association (1995) *Code of Ethics and Standards of Practice.* Alexandria, VA: ACA.

American Counseling Association (2014) *Code of Ethics and Standards of Practice.* Alexandria, VA: ACA.

American Psychological Association (1992) *Ethical Principles of Psychologists and Code of Conduct.* Washington, DC: APA.

American Psychological Association (2017) *Ethical Principles of Psychologists and Code of Conduct.* Washington, DC: APA.

Andrews, N., Kim, S., & Watanabe, J. (2018) Cultural humility as a transformative framework for librarians, tutors, and youth volunteers: applying a lens of cultural responsiveness in training library staff and volunteers. *Young Adult Library Services, 16*(2), 19.

Aponte, J.F., Rivers, Y.R., & Wohl, J. (1995) *Psychological Interventions and Cultural Diversity.* Needham Heights, MA: Allyn & Bacon.

Arredondo, P. (1999) Multicultural counseling competencies as tools to address oppression and racism. *Journal of Counseling and Development*, *77*(1), 102–108.

Avrahami, D. (2006) Visual art therapy's unique contribution in the treatment of post-traumatic stress disorders. *Journal of Trauma & Dissociation*, *6*(4), 5–38.

Awais, Y.J., & Yali, A.M. (2013) A call for diversity: the need to recruit and retain ethnic minority students in art therapy. *Art Therapy: Journal of the American Art Therapy Association*, *30*(3), 130–134.

Bal, J., & Kaur, R. (2018) Cultural humility in art therapy and child and youth care: reflections on practice by Sikh women (L'humilité culturelle en art-thérapie et les soins aux enfants et aux jeunes: réflexions sur la pratique de femmes sikhes). *Canadian Art Therapy Association Journal*, *31*(1), 6.

Bent-Goodley, T. (2001) Eradicating domestic violence in the African American community. *Trauma, Violence & Abuse*, *2*(4), 316–330.

Betancourt, J.R., Green, A. R., Carrillo, E. J., & Ananeh-Firempong, O. (2003) Defining cultural competence: a practical framework for addressing racial/ethnic disparities in health and health care. *Public Health Reports*, *118*(4), 293–302.

Bethea-Whitfield, P., Harley, D., & Dillard, J. (2005) *African American Women and Mental Health: Contemporary Mental Health Issues among African Americans.* Alexandria, VA: American Counseling Association.

Black, M.C., Basile, K.C., Breiding, M.J., Smith, S.G., et al. (2011) *The National Intimate Partner and Sexual Violence Survey (NISVS): 2010 Summary Report.* Atlanta, GA: National Center for Injury Prevention and Control, Centers for Disease Control and Prevention.

Bodlovic, A., & Jackson, L. (2018) A cultural humility approach to art therapy multicultural pedagogy: barriers to compassion. *The International Journal of Diversity in Education*, *19*(1), 1–9.

Bolman, L., & Deal, T. (2008) *Reframing Organizations: Artistry, Choice and Leadership* (4th ed.). Hoboken, NJ: Jossey-Bass & Pfeiffer Imprints, Wiley.

Bone, T.A. (2018) Art and mental health recovery: evaluating the impact of a community-based participatory arts program through artist voices. *Community Mental Health Journal*, *8*, 1180.

Boston, C. (2014) My Identity: A Mosaic Design. In M.B. Junge (ed.), *Identity and Art Therapy: Personal and Professional Perspectives* (pp.58–72). Springfield, IL: Charles C. Thomas.

Boston, C., & Short, G. (1998) Art Therapy: An Afrocentric Approach. In A.R. Hiscox & A.C. Calisch (eds.) *Tapestry of Cultural Issues in Art Therapy.* London: Jessica Kingsley Publishers.

Boston, C., & Short, G. (2006) Notes, Georgette Seabrook Powell. *Art Therapy: Journal of the American Art Therapy, Association, 23*(2), 89–90.

Boston, C.G. (2005) Life story of an art therapist of color. *Art Therapy: Journal of the American Art Therapy Association, 22*(4), 189–192.

Brems, C., & Rasmussen, C.H. (2019) *A Comprehensive Guide to Child Psychotherapy and Counseling.* Long Grove, IL: Waveland Press.

British Association of Art Therapists (2014) *Code of Ethics and Principles of Professional Practice for Art Therapists.* London: BAAT.

California Association of Marriage and Family Therapists (2004) *Code of Ethics.* San Diego, CA: CAMFT.

California Association of Marriage and Family Therapists (2011) *Code of Ethics.* San Diego, CA: CAMFT.

Calisch, A. (2003) Multicultural training and art therapy: past, present and future. *Art Therapy: Journal of the American Art Therapy Association, 20*(1), 11–15.

Campbell, J., Liebmann, M., Brooks, F., Jones, J., & Ward, C. (1999) *Art Therapy, Race and Culture.* London: Jessica Kingsley Publishers.

Carey, L. (2006) *Expressive and Creative Arts Methods for Trauma Survivors.* London: Jessica Kingsley Publishers.

Castle, M.C. (2001) Interpreters, docents and educators: ways of knowing, ways of teaching in a history museum, an art gallery, and a nature centre. Qualitative research thesis, Ontario Institute for Studies in Education of the University of Toronto.

Centers for Disease Control and Prevention (2018) Intimate partner violence. Accessed on 08/05/2019 at www.cdc.gov/violenceprevention/intimatepartnerviolence/index.html.

Cherry, L.A. (2002) Multigroup ethnic identity measure with art therapy students: assessing preservice students after one multicultural self-reflection course. *Art Therapy: Journal of the American Art Therapy Association, 19*(4), 159–163.

Chilcote, R.L. (2007) Art therapy with child tsunami survivors in Sri Lanka. *Art Therapy: Journal of the American Art Therapy Association, 24*(4), 154–155.

Collins, P.H. (2002) *Black Feminist Thought: Knowledge, Consciousness, and the Politics of Empowerment.* New York: Routledge.

Corey, G., Corey, M.S., & Callanan, P. (2003) *Issues and Ethics in the Helping Professions* (6th ed.). Pacific Grove, CA: Brooks/Cole.

Danso, R. (2018) Cultural competence and cultural humility: a critical reflection on key cultural diversity concepts. *Journal of Social Work, 18*(4), 410.

David, P. (2008) Collectivist societies & mental health treatment. Accessed on 08/05/2019 at http://pauldavidphd.com/wp-content/uploads/Collectivist-Article.pdf.

de Botton, A., & Armstrong, J. (2013) *Art as Therapy*. London: Phaidon Press.

De Luca, V. (2015) Art is life: editorial, *Essence Magazine, 46*(14), 8.

Dissanayake, E. (1995) *Homoaestheticus: Where Art Comes from and Why*. Seattle, WA: University of Washington Press.

Doby-Copeland, C. (2006a) Cultural diversity curriculum design: an art therapist's perspective. *Art Therapy: Journal of the American Art Therapy Association, 23*(4), 172–180.

Doby-Copeland, C. (2006b) Things come to me: reflections from an art therapist of color. *Art Therapy: Journal of the American Art Therapy Association, 23*(2), 81–85.

Dokter, D. (1998) *Arts Therapists, Refugees, and Migrants: Reaching across Borders*. London: Jessica Kingsley Publishers.

Donnelly, D.A., Cook, K.J., Van Ausdale, D., & Foley, L. (2005) White privilege, color blindness, and services to battered women. *Violence Against Women, 11*(1), 6–37.

Dreikurs, R. (1971) *The Scientific Revolution: Social Equality: The Challenge of Today*. Chicago, IL: The Alfred Adler Institute.

Dye, L. (2017) *Using Art Techniques across Cultural and Race Boundaries: Working with Identity*. London: Jessica Kingsley Publishers.

Elkins, D.E., & Deaver, S.P. (2013) American Art Therapy Association, Inc.: 2011 membership survey report. *Art Therapy: Journal of the American Art Therapy Association, 30*(1), 36–45.

Elmendorf, D. (2010) Minding our p's through q's: addressing possibilities and precautions of community work through new questions. *Art Therapy: Journal of the American Art Therapy Association, 27*(1), 40–43.

Elsayed, D., & Ahmed, R. (2009) Medical ethics: what is it? Why is it important? *Sudanese Journal of Public Health, 4*(1), 284–287.

Engstrom, D., Hernández, P., & Gangsei, D. (2008) Vicarious resilience: a qualitative investigation into its description. *Traumatology, 14*(3), 13–21.

Farris, P. (2006) Mentors of diversity. *Art Therapy: Journal of the American Art Therapy Association, 23*(2), 86–88.

Feen-Calligan, H., Moreno, J., & Buzzard, E. (2018) Art therapy, community building, activism, and outcomes. *Frontiers in Psychology, 9*, 1548.

Fincher, S. (1991) *Creating Mandalas: For Insight, Healing and Self-Expression*. Boston, MA: Shambhala.

Fincher, S. (2009) *The Mandala Workbook: A Creative Guide for Self-Exploration, Balance and Well-Being*. Boston, MA: Shambhala.

Fish, B.J. (2012) Response art: the art of the art therapist. *Art Therapy: Journal of the American Art Therapy Association, 29*(3), 138–143.

Fobear, K. (2017) "This painting is nice, but I wish it were more political." Exploring the challenges and dilemmas of community art with LGBT refugees. *Women's Studies International Forum, 62*, 52–60.

Forrest-Bank, S., Nicotera, N., Bassett, D., & Ferrarone, P. (2016) Effects of an expressive art intervention with urban youth in low-income neighborhoods. *Child & Adolescent Social Work Journal, 33*(5), 429–441.

Freire, P. (1970) *Pedagogy of the Oppressed.* New York: Bloomsbury.

Frostig, K. (2011) Arts activism: praxis in social justice, critical discourse, and radical modes of engagement. *Art Therapy: Journal of the American Art Therapy Association, 28*(2), 50–56.

Furman, L., & Boeve, H. (2018) Itinerant art therapy: an educational model for community outreach therapeutic service. *The Arts in Psychotherapy, 57*, 65–71.

Gallardo, M.E. (2014) *Developing Cultural Humility: Embracing Race, Privilege and Power.* Los Angeles, CA: SAGE.

George, J., Greene, B.D., & Blackwell, M. (2005) Three voices on multiculturalism in the art therapy classroom. *Art Therapy: Journal of the American Art Therapy Association, 22*(3), 132–138.

Gerber, N. (2014) The Therapist Artist: An Individual and Collective Worldview. In M. Junge (ed.) *The Identity of the Art Therapist* (pp.85–95). Springfield, IL: Charles C. Thomas.

Gergen, K.J. (2000) Psychological science in a postmodern context. *The American Psychologist, 56*(10), 803–813.

Gerity, L.A. (2000) The subversive art therapist: embracing cultural diversity in the art room. *Art Therapy: Journal of the American Art Therapy Association, 17*(3), 202–206.

Gipson, L.R. (2015) Is cultural competence enough? Deepening social justice pedagogy in art therapy. *Art Therapy, 32*(3), 142–145.

Gipson, L. (2019) Envisioning Black Women's Consciousness in Art Therapy. In S.K. Talwar, *Art Therapy for Social Justice: Radical Intersections* (pp.96–120). New York: Routledge.

Golub, D. (2005) Social action art therapy. *Art Therapy: Journal of the American Art Therapy Association, 22*(1), 17–23.

Gómez Carlier, N., & Salom, A. (2012) When art therapy migrates: the acculturation challenge of sojourner art therapists. *Art Therapy: Journal of the American Art Therapy Association, 29*(1), 4–10.

Google Dictionary (n.d. a) Bias. Accessed on 08/26/2019 at www.google.com/search?client=safari&rls=en&q=bias+definition&ie=UTF-8&oe=UTF-8.

Google Dictionary (n.d. b) Assumption. Accessed on 08/26/2019 at www.google.com/search?client=safari&rls=en&q=assumption+definition&ie=UTF-8&oe=UTF-8.

Hackling, S., Secker, J., Spandler, H., Kent, L., & Shenton, J.O. (2008) Evaluating the impact of participatory arts projects for people with mental health needs. *Health and Social Care in the Community, 16*(6), 638–648.

Hampton, R., Oliver, W., & Magarian, L. (2003) Domestic violence in the African American community: an analysis of social and structural factors. *Violence Against Women, 9*(5), 533–557.

Hamrick, C., & Byma, C. (2017) Know history, know self: art therapists' responsibility to dismantle white supremacy. *Art Therapy: Journal of the American Art Therapy Association, 34*(3), 106–111.

Hanania, A. (2018) A proposal for culturally informed art therapy with Syrian refugee women: the potential for trauma expression through embroidery (Une proposition d'art-thérapie adaptée à la culture de femmes réfugiées syriennes: le potentiel de la broderie pour l'expression du traumatisme). *Canadian Art Therapy Association Journal, 31*(1), 33.

Har-Gil, O. (2010) Cultural humility in art therapy: an heuristic arts-based inquiry. Unpublished graduate project, non-thesis.

Hass-Cohen, N., & Carr, R. (2008) *Art Therapy and Clinical Neuroscience.* London: Jessica Kingsley Publishers.

Hays, P. (2001) Becoming a Culturally Responsive Therapist. In P. Hays (ed.) *Addressing Cultural Complexities in Practice: A Framework for Clinicians and Counselors* (pp.19–34). Washington, DC: American Psychological Association.

Helguera, P. (2011) *Educator for Socially Engaged Art.* New York: Jorge Pinto Books.

Henley, D.R. (1999) Questioning multiculturalism in art therapy: problems with political correctness and censorship. *Art Therapy: Journal of the American Art Therapy Association, 16*(3), 140.

Hernandez, P., Engstrom, D., & Gangsei, D., (2010) Exploring the impact of trauma on the therapist: vicarious resilience and related concepts in training. *Journal of Systemic Therapies, 29*(1), 67–83.

Hiscox, A.R., & Calisch, A.C. (eds.) (1998) *Tapestry of Cultural Issues in Art Therapy.* London: Jessica Kingsley Publishers.

Hocoy, D. (2002) Cross-cultural issues in art therapy. *Art Therapy: Journal of the American Art Therapy Association, 19*(4), 141–145.

Hocoy, D. (2005) Art therapy and social action: a transpersonal framework. *Art Therapy: Journal of the American Art Therapy Association, 22*(1), 7–16.

Hocoy, D. (2006) Art therapy: working in the borderlands. *Art Therapy: Journal of the American Art Therapy Association, 23*(3), 132–135.

Hogan, S. (2016) *Art Therapy Theories: A Critical Introduction*. London: Routledge.

Hogan, S., & Pink, S. (2010) Routes to interiorities: art therapy and knowing in anthropology. *Visual Anthropology, 23*(2), 158–174.

Hook, J., Boan, D., Davis, D., Aten, J., Ruiz, J., & Maryon, T. (2016) Cultural humility and hospital safety culture. *Journal of Clinical Psychology in Medical Settings, 23*(4), 402–409.

Hook, J.N., Davis, D.E., Owen, J., Worthington, E.L. Jr., & Utsey, S.O. (2013) Cultural humility: measuring openness to culturally diverse clients. *Journal of Counseling Psychology, 60*(3), 353.

hooks, b. (1993) *Sisters of the Yam: Black Women and Self-Recovery*. London: Turnaround.

Howells, V., & Zelnick, T. (2009) Making art: a qualitative study of personal and group transformation in a community arts studio. *Psychiatric Rehabilitation Journal, 32*(3), 215–222.

Howie, P., Prasad, S., & Kristel, J. (2013) *Using Art Therapy with Diverse Populations: Crossing Cultures and Abilities*. London: Jessica Kingsley Publishers.

Huss, E. (2009) "A coat of many colors": towards an integrative multilayered model of art therapy. *The Arts in Psychotherapy, 36*(3), 154–160.

Huss, E. (2018) Arts as a methodology for connecting between micro and macro knowledge in social work: examples of impoverished Bedouin women's images in Israel. *British Journal of Social Work, 48*(1), 73.

Iqbal, A. (2015) The ethical considerations of counseling psychologists working with trauma. *Counseling Psychology Review, 30*(1), 44–51.

İsmail, N., & Tekke, M. (2015) Rediscovering Rogers's self theory and personality. *Journal of Educational, Health and Community Psychology, 4*(3), 2088–3129.

Itzel Marquez, C. (2018) A heuristic exploration of the multidimensional experiences of a xicana art therapist in-training working in her community. Unpublished thesis, Loyola Marymount University, Los Angeles.

Jackson, L. (2016) Acquiring new knowledge through art self-exploration and collective journaling to enhance cultural humility in art therapy. Doctoral dissertation, Proquest LLC.

Jackson, L., & Metzl, E. (2017) Cultural fabrics of self, family & community. Expressive Arts Therapies Summit, Los Angeles, CA.

Jackson, L., & Metzl, E. (2017) Between me and we: personal and collective informed by cultural humility. Expressive Arts Therapies Summit, Los Angeles, CA.

Jackson, L., Mezzera, C., & Satterberg, M. (2018) Wisdom Through Diversity in Art Therapy. In R. Carolan, & A. Backos (eds.) *Emerging Perspectives in*

*Art Therapy: Trends, Movements, and Developments* (pp. 105–122). New York: Routledge.

Joseph, C. (2006) Creative alliance: the healing power of art therapy. *Art Therapy: Journal of the American Art Therapy Association, 23*(1), 30–33.

Jun, H. (2010) *Social Justice, Multicultural Counseling and Practice beyond a Conventional Approach.* Los Angeles, CA: SAGE.

Junge, M.B. (2014) *Identity and Art Therapy: Personal and Professional Perspectives.* Springfield, IL: Charles C. Thomas.

Kalmanowitz, D., & Ho, R.T.H. (2016) Out of our mind: art therapy and mindfulness with refugees, political violence and trauma. *The Arts in Psychotherapy, 49*(2), 57–65.

Kapitan, L. (2010) *Introduction to Art Therapy Research.* New York: Routledge Taylor & Francis.

Kapitan, L. (2012) Educating the future practitioner of art therapy. *Art Therapy: Journal of the American Art Therapy Association, 29*(4), 148–149.

Kapitan, L. (2015) Social action in practice: shifting the ethnocentric lens in cross-cultural art therapy encounters. *Art Therapy: Journal of the American Art Therapy Association, 32*(3), 104–111.

Kapitan, L., Litell, M., & Torres, A. (2011) Creative art therapy in a community's participatory research and social transformation. *Art Therapy: Journal of the American Art Therapy Association, 28*(2), 64–73.

Karcher, O.P. (2017) Sociopolitical oppression, trauma, and healing: moving toward a social justice art therapy framework. *Art Therapy: Journal of the American Art Therapy Association, 34*(3), 123.

Keselman, M., & Awais, Y.J. (2018) Exploration of cultural humility in medical art therapy. *Art Therapy: Journal of the American Art Therapy Association, 35*(2), 77–87.

Kerr, C. (2015) *Multicultural Family Art Therapy.* New York: Routledge.

Kramer, E. (1986) The art therapist's third hand: reflections on art, art therapy, and society at large. *American Journal of Art Therapy, 24*(3), 71–86.

Kuri, E. (2017) Toward an ethical application of intersectionality in art therapy. *Art Therapy: Journal of the American Art Therapy Association, 34*(3), 118–122.

LaFrance, J., & Blizzard, J. (2013) Student perceptions of digital story telling as a learning-tool for educational leaders. *International Journal of Educational Leadership Preparation, 8*(2), 25–43.

Lambert, D., Donahue, A., Mitchell, M., & Strauss, R. (2001) *Mental Health Outreach: Promising Practices in Rural Areas.* Washington, DC: National Association for Rural Mental Health.

Lavery, T.P. (1994) Culture shock: adventuring into the inner city through post-session imagery. *American Journal of Art Therapy, 33*(1), 14.

Levine, E.G., & Levine, S.K. (2011) *Art in Action: Expressive Art Therapy and Social Change*. London: Jessica Kingsley Publishers.

Levy, S. (2006) Your daddy is the boogeyman. *Art Therapy: Journal of the American Art Therapy Association, 23*(3), 136–138.

Lewis, P. (1997) Transpersonal arts psychotherapy: toward an ecumenical worldview. *The Arts in Psychotherapy, 24*(3), 243–254.

Liebmann, M., & Weston, S. (2015) *Art Therapy with Physical Conditions*. London: Jessica Kingsley Publishers.

Linesch, D., & Carnay, J. (2005) Short communication: supporting cultural competency in art therapy training. *The Arts in Psychotherapy, 32*(5), 382–394.

Linesch, D.B., Metzl, E., & Treviño, A.L. (2015) Various aspects of art therapy in Mexico/Algunos aspectos de la terapia de arte en México. Digital Commons at Loyola Marymount University and Loyola Law School.

Lopez-Littleton, V., & Burr, J. (2018) A move towards cultural humility in the public sector. *PATimes*, American Society for Public Administration. Accessed on 08/27/2019 at https://patimes.org/a-move-towards-cultural-humility-in-the-public-sector.

Loue, S. (2018) Using sociodrama to foster cultural humility among faculty and students in the academic medical center. *Romanian Journal for Multidimensional Education/Revista Romaneasca Pentru Educatie Multidimensionala, 10*(2), 45–57.

Lumpkin, C.L. (2006) Relating cultural identity and identity as art therapist. *Journal of the American Art Therapy Association, 23*(1), 34–38.

Lynch, R.T., & Chosa, D. (1996) Group-oriented community-based expressive arts programming for individuals with disabilities. *Journal of Rehabilitation, 62*(3), 75.

Maat, M.B. (1997) A group art therapy experience for immigrant adolescents. *American Journal of Art Therapy, 36*(1), 11.

Macleod, R.M. (1975) Scientific advice for British India: imperial perceptions and administrative goals, 1898–1923. *Modern Asian Studies, 9*(3), 343–384.

Malchiodi, C.A. (1997) Invasive Art: Art as Empowerment for Women with Breast Cancer. In S. Hogan (ed.) *Feminist Approaches to Art Therapy* (pp.49–64). London: Routledge.

Mama, A. (1995) *Beyond the Masks – Race, Gender and Subjectivity*. London: Routledge.

Martin, R., & Barresi, J. (2006) *The Rise and Fall of Soul and Self: An Intellectual History of Personal Identity*. New York: Columbia University Press.

Martin, R., & Barresi, J. (2008) *The Rise and Fall of Soul and Self: An Intellectual History of Personal Identity*. West Sussex, NY: Columbia University Press.

Maslow, A.H. (1943) A theory of human motivation. *Psychological Review,* 50(4), 370–396.

Masuria, M. (2012) "Procrastination, theft of time..." Accessed on 8/1/2019 at https://plugintosource.wordpress.com/2012/01/20/procrastination-theft-of-time.

McGann, E.P. (2006) Color me beautiful: racism, identity formation, and art therapy. *Journal of Emotional Abuse,* 6(2/3), 197.

McNiff, S. (1993) The authority of experience. *The Arts in Psychotherapy, 20,* 3–9.

McNiff, S. (1998) *Art Based Research.* London: Jessica Kingsley Publishers.

McNiff, S. (2009) Cross-cultural psychotherapy and art. *Art Therapy: Journal of the American Art Therapy Association,* 26(3), 100–106.

Merriam-Webster (2019a) Arrogance. *Merriam-Webster's Online Dictionary.* Accessed on 08/05/2019 at www.merriam- webster.com/dictionary/arrogance#learn-more.

Merriam-Webster (2019b) Assumption. *Merriam-Webster's Online Dictionary.* Accessed on 08/05/2019 at www.merriam-webster.com/dictionary/assumption.

Merriam-Webster (2019c) Belief. *Merriam-Webster's Online Dictionary.* Accessed on 08/05/2019 at www.merriam-webster.com/dictionary/belief.

Merriam-Webster (2019d) Bias. *Merriam-Webster's Online Dictionary.* Accessed on 08/05/2019 at www.merriam-webster.com/dictionary/bias.

Merriam-Webster (2019e) Variable. *Merriam-Webster's Online Dictionary.* Accessed on 08/23/2019 at www.merriam-webster.com/dictionary/variable.

Milner, F. (2004) *Frida Kahlo.* London: PRC Publications.

Moon, B.L. (2015) *Ethical Issues in Art Therapy* (3rd ed.). Springfield, IL: Charles C. Thomas.

Myers, L.J. (1988) *Understanding an Afrocentric World View: Introduction to an Optimal Psychology* (2nd ed.). Dubuque, IA: Kendall/Hunt.

Nicolaidis, C., Timmons, V., Thomas, M.J., Waters, A.S., *et al.* (2010) "You don't go 'tell white people nothing": African American women's perspectives on the influence of violence and race on depression and depression care. *American Journal of Public Health,* 100(8), 1470–1476.

Nolan, E. (2013) Common ground of two paradigms: incorporating critical theory into current art therapy practices. *Art Therapy: Journal of the American Art Therapy Association,* 30(4), 177–180.

Nonaka, I. (1991) The knowledge-creating company. *Harvard Business Review,* November–December, 96–104.

Nonaka, I., & Takeuchi, H. (1995) *The Knowledge-Creating Company: How Japanese Companies Create the Dynamics of Innovation.* Oxford: Oxford University Press.

Ordway, B. (2018) A heuristic exploration of the intersections of social justice theory, community art therapy, and cultural humility. Digital Commons at Loyola Marymount University and Loyola Law School.

Ottemiller, D.D., & Awais, Y.J. (2016) A model for art therapists in community-based practice. *Art Therapy: Journal of The American Art Therapy Association*, *33*(3), 144–150.

Park, B. (2017) A Korean art therapist's autoethnography concerning re-acculturation to the motherland following training in the UK. *International Journal of Art Therapy: Inscape*, *22*(4), 154.

Partridge, E. (2019) *Art Therapy with Older Adults*. London: Jessica Kingsley Publishers.

Paz, O. (1991) *The Labyrinth of Solitude and the Other Mexico: Return to the Labyrinth of Solitude; Mexico and the United States; the Philanthropic Ogre.* New York: Grove Press.

Pedersen, P. (2000) *A Handbook for Developing Multicultural Awareness.* Alexandra, VA: American Counseling Association.

Pelton-Sweet, L.M., & Sherry, A. (2008) Coming out through art: a review of art therapy with LGBT clients. *Art Therapy: Journal of the American Art Therapy Association*, *25*(4), 170–176.

Pitesa, M., & Thau, S. (2014) A lack of material resources causes harsher moral judgments. *Psychological Science*, *25*(3), 702–710.

Potash, J. (2005) Rekindling the multicultural history of the American Art Therapy Association Inc. *Art Therapy: Journal of the American Art Therapy Association*, *22*(4), 184–188.

Potash, J. (2011) Art therapists as intermediaries for social change. *Journal of Art for Life*, *2*(1), 48.

Potash, J. (2018) Relational social justice ethics for art therapists. *Art Therapy, Journal of the American Art Therapy Association*, *35*(4), 202–210.

Potash, J., & Ramirez, W. (2013) Broadening history, expanding possibilities: contributions of Wayne Ramirez to art therapy. *Art Therapy: Journal of the American Art Therapy Association*, *30*(4), 169–176.

Potash, J.S., Bardot, H., Moon, C.H., Napoli, M., Lyonsmith, A., & Hamilton, M. (2017) Ethical implications of cross-cultural international art therapy. *The Arts in Psychotherapy*, *56*, 74–82.

Potash, J.S., Chan, S.M., & Kalmanowitz, D.L. (2012) *Art Therapy in Asia: To the Bone or Wrapped in Silk*. London: Jessica Kingsley Publishers.

Potash, J.S., Doby-Copeland, C., Stepney, S.A., Washington, B.N., *et al.* (2015) Advancing Multicultural and diversity competence in art therapy: American Art Therapy Association Multicultural Committee 1990–2015. *Art Therapy: Journal of the American Art Therapy Association*, *32*(3), 146–150.

Potash, J., & Gymiah-Boadi, A. (2018) Arts-based civic dialogues in politically charged time. Annual Conference of the American Art Therapy Association, Miami, FL.

Ray, T. (2009) Rethinking Polanyi's concept of tacit knowledge: from personal knowing to imagined institutions. *Minerva, 47*(1), 75–92.

Reim Ifrach, E., & Miller, A. (2016) Social action art therapy as an intervention for compassion fatigue. *The Arts in Psychotherapy, 50,* 34–39.

Robb, M. (2012) The history of art therapy at the national institutes of health. *Art Therapy: Journal of the American Art Therapy Association, 29*(1), 33–37.

Roberts, R., Phinney, J., Masse, L., Chen, Y.R., Roberts, C., and Romero, A. (1999) Multi Ethnic Identity Measure. *Journal of Early Adolescence, 19*(3), 301–322.

Rosenberg, M.B. (2003) *Nonviolent Communication: A Language of Life* (2nd ed.). Encinitas, CA: Puddledancer Press.

Rossetto, E. (2012) A hermeneutic phenomenological study of community mural making and social action art therapy. *Art Therapy: Journal of the American Art Therapy Association, 29*(1), 19–26.

Rubin, J.A. (2001) *Approaches to Art Therapy: Theory and Technique* (2nd ed.). Philadelphia: Brunner-Routledge.

Sadeghi, M., Fischer, J.M., & House, S.G. (2003) Ethical dilemmas in multicultural counseling. *Journal of Multicultural Counseling and Development, 31*(3), 179–191.

Sajnani, N., Marxen, E., & Zarate, R. (2017) Critical perspectives in the arts therapies: response/ability across a continuum of practice. *The Arts in Psychotherapy, 54,* 28–37.

Schouten, K.A., de Niet, G.J., Knipscheer, J.W., Kleber, R.J., & Hutschemaekers, G.J. (2015) The effectiveness of art therapy in the treatment of traumatized adults: a systematic review on art therapy and trauma. *Trauma Violence Abuse, 16*(2), 220–228.

Shottenkirk, D. (2007) Research, relativism, and truth in art. *Glasgow School of Art E-journal, 1*(1), 1–6.

Slayton, S.C. (2012) Building community as social action: an art therapy group with adolescent males. *The Arts In Psychotherapy, 39*(3), 179–185.

Speight, S.L., Myers, L.J., Cox, C.I., & Highlen, P.S. (1991) A redefinition of multicultural counseling. *Journal of Counseling and Development, 70*(1), 29–36.

Springham, N. (2008) Through the eyes of the law: what is it about art that can harm people? *International Journal of Art Therapy: Inscape, 13*(2), 65.

Staats, C. (2014) State of the science: implicit bias review 2014. Accessed on 08/27/2019 at http://kirwaninstitute.osu.edu/wp-content/uploads/2014/03/2014-implicit-bias.pdf.

Storm, E. (2001) *Art, Culture and the National Agenda, Strengthening Communities through Culture.* Washington, DC: Americans for the Arts (formerly Center for Arts and Culture).

Sue, D.W. (2001) Multidimensional facets of cultural competence. *The Counseling Psychologist, 29*(6), 790–821.

Sue, D.W., & Sue, D. (1999) *Counseling the Culturally Different: Theory and Practice* (3rd ed.). Hoboken, NJ: John Wiley & Sons.

Sue, D.W., & Sue, D. (2008) *Counseling the Culturally Different: Theory and Practice* (5th ed.). Hoboken, NJ: John Wiley & Sons.

Sutherland, I., & Acord, S.K. (2007) Thinking with art: from situated knowledge to experiential knowing. *Journal of Visual Art Practice, 6*(2), 125–140.

Talwar, S. (2010) An intersectional framework for race, class, gender, and sexuality in art therapy. *Art Therapy: Journal of the American Art Therapy Association, 27*(1), 11–17.

Talwar, S. (2015) Culture, diversity, and identity: from margins to center. *Art Therapy: Journal of the American Art Therapy Association, 32*(3), 100–103.

Talwar, S. (2017) Ethics, law, and cultural competence in art therapy. *Art Therapy: Journal of the American Art Therapy Association, 34*(3), 102.

Talwar, S., Iyer, J., & Doby-Copeland, C. (2004) The invisible veil: changing paradigms in the art therapy profession. *Art Therapy: Journal of the American Art Therapy Association, 21*(1), 44–48.

Talwar, S.K. (2019) *Art Therapy for Social Justice: Radical Intersections.* New York: Routledge.

ter Maat, M.B. (2011) Developing and assessing multicultural competence with a focus on culture and ethnicity. *Art Therapy: Journal of the American Art Therapy Association, 28*(1), 4–10.

Tervalon, M. (2012) Cultural humility training. County of San Mateo, San Mateo, CA [training].

Tervalon, M. (2015) Cultural humility training. Working in Partnership with Individuals, Families and Communities, Symposium, Daly City, Serramonte del Rey, October.

Tervalon, M., & Lewis, L. (2018) Cultural humility: working in partnership with individuals, families and communities. Training the Trainer Workshop, Oakland, CA.

Tervalon, M., & Murray-Garcia, J. (1998) Cultural humility versus cultural competence: a critical distinction in defining physician training outcomes in multicultural education. *Journal of Health Care for the Poor and Underserved, 9*(2), 117–125.

Thompson, M.P., Kaslow, N.J., Kingree, J.B., Rashid, A., *et al.* (2000) Partner violence, social support, and distress among inner-city African American women. *American Journal of Community Psychology, 28*(1), 127–140.

Tillet, S., & Tillet, S. (2019) "You want to be well?" Self-Care as a Black Feminist Intervention in Art Therapy. In S.K. Talwar (ed.) *Art Therapy for Social Justice: Radical Intersections* (pp.123–143). New York: Routledge.

Timm-Bottos, J. (2011) Endangered threads: socially committed community art action. *Art Therapy, 28*(2), 57–63.

Timm-Bottos, J. (2017) Public practice art therapy: enabling spaces across North America (La pratique publique de l'art-thérapie: des espaces habilitants partout en Amérique du Nord). *Canadian Art Therapy Association Journal, 30*(2), 94.

Tisdell, E.J., Gupta, K., Archuleta, K., Velott, D., & Sprow Forte, K. (2019) Toward health equity: mindfulness and cultural humility as adult education. *New Directions for Adult and Continuing Education, 161*, 57–66.

Trommsdorff, G. (2002) An Eco-Cultural and Interpersonal Relations Approach to Development of the Lifespan. In W.J. Lonner, D.L. Dinnel, S.A. Hayes, & D.N. Sattler (eds.) *Online Readings in Psychology and Culture* (Unit 12, Chapter 1). Center for Cross-Cultural Research, Western Washington University, Bellingham, Washington, DC.

Van der Kolk, B.A. (1994) The body keeps the score: memory and the evolving psychobiology of posttraumatic stress. *Harvard Review of Psychiatry, 1*(5), 253–265.

Van der Kolk, B.A., & Fisler, R. (1995) Dissociation and the fragmentary nature of traumatic memories: overview and exploratory study. *Journal of Traumatic Stress, 8*(4), 505–525.

Venture, L. (1977) The Black beat in art therapy experiences. Unpublished dissertation, Union Institute (formally Union Graduate School), Cincinnati, OH.

Vick, R.M., & Sexton-Radek, K. (2008) Community-based art studios in Europe and the United States: a comparative study. *Art Therapy: Journal of the American Art Therapy Association, 25*(1), 4–10.

Watch Cut Video. (Producer) (2016) *One Word Series Episode 36: Angry Black Woman* [Video file]. Accessed on 08/05/2019 at www.youtube.com/watch?v=0xRPxQEEzI4&list=PLJic7bfGlo3p3MZQ28prCQxWSZQTytqF8& index=36.

Weinberg, T. (2018) Gaining cultural competence through alliances in art therapy with indigenous clients (La compétence culturelle et son acquisition grâce à des alliances avec des clients autochtones en art-thérapie). *Canadian Art Therapy Association Journal, 31*(1), 14.

Wildman, P., & Inayatullah, S. (1996) Ways of knowing, culture, communication and the pedagogies of the future. *Futures*, *28*(8), 723–740.

Winnicott, D.W. (1960) Ego Distortion in Terms of True and False Self (pp.140–152). In *The Maturational Process and the Facilitating Environment: Studies in the Theory of Emotional Development*. New York: International UP.

Yeager, K., & Bauer-Wu, S. (2013) Cultural humility: essential foundation for clinical researchers. *Applied Nursing Research*, *26*(4), 251–256.

Yedidia, T., & Lipschitz-Elchawi, R. (2012) Examining social perceptions between Arab and Jewish children through human figure drawings. *Art Therapy: Journal of the American Art Therapy Association*, *29*(3), 104.

Yeung, A.S., Trinh, N.-H.T., Chen, J.A., Chang, T.E., & Stern, T.A. (2018) Perspective: cultural humility for consultation-liaison psychiatrists. *Psychosomatics*, *59*(6), 554–560.

# Subject Index

# Author Index